HOW TO PLAY ROCK GUITAR

THE BASICS & BEYOND

LEAD · RHYTHM · GEAR · RECORDING & MORE!

By the Editors of *Guitar Player*

Backbeat
Books
San Francisco

Published by Backbeat Books
600 Harrison Street, San Francisco, CA 94107
www.backbeatbooks.com
email: books@musicplayer.com

An imprint of the Music Player Group
Publishers of *Guitar Player, Bass Player, Keyboard*, and other magazines
United Entertainment Media, Inc.
A CMP Information company

CMP
United Business Media

Distributed to the book trade in the US and Canada by
Publishers Group West, 1700 Fourth Street, Berkeley, CA 94710

Distributed to the music trade in the US and Canada by
Hal Leonard Publishing, Box 13819, Milwaukee, WI 53213

Edited by Richard Johnston
Cover and Text Design: Richard Leeds – bigwigdesign.com

Library of Congress Cataloging-in-Publication Data

How to play rock guitar : the basics & beyond : lead, rhythm, gear, recording & more / edited by Richard Johnston.– Rev. and expanded.
        p. cm. – (Guitar player musician's library)
    "Includes 12 free audio lessons online"–Cover, CIP galley.
    Discography: p.
    ISBN 0-87930-740-4 (alk. paper)
    1. Guitar–Instruction and study. 2. Rock music–Instruction and study. I. Johnston,
Richard, 1947– II. Guitar player. III. Series.

MT580 .H8195 2003
787.87'166143–dc21

                                                                          2002038357

Printed in the United States of America
03 04 05 06 07   5 4 3 2 1

Contents

Introduction to the Second Edition

A music professor of mine possessed possibly the most bipolar record collection I've ever encountered. Within his long rows of LPs, Beethoven jostled Bowie, Deep Purple crowded Debussy, Led Zeppelin cozied up to Lutoslawski. The common theme, this academic maintained, was the all-embracing nature of the two forms—both classical and rock musicians tend to scoop up whatever's around and make it their own, creating new sounds along the way.

The history of rock guitar bears out his theory, whether it's Paul Burlison putting a boogie beat to hillbilly music and Memphis blues, Eric Clapton supercharging riffs from Robert Johnson and Muddy Waters, or Eddie Van Halen melding his classical-piano background with his love of Clapton and Page—and forging guitar techniques that players such as Yngwie Malmsteen would later apply to classical compositions. One of rock guitar's most explosive amalgamations has occurred in the few years since the initial publication of *How to Play Rock Guitar*, with players such as Rage Against the Machine's Tom Morello creating a meltdown fusion of funk, punk, and metal.

Since the heyday of Jimi Hendrix, *Guitar Player* magazine has explored the work of rock's boldest innovators, while keeping its readers in touch with the instrument's history. For this second edition of *How to Play Rock Guitar* I've taken some of the best *GP* lessons of the past few years and mixed them with classics from the first edition—including a session with Eddie Van Halen himself—to reveal the secrets of rock guitar's heroes, from the rockabilly pioneers of the '50s to the rap-metal monsters of the early 21st century. As always in *Guitar Player*, you'll learn techniques directly from top players, and you'll gain vital information on their equipment and their sources of inspiration. You'll also be able to hear the lessons online, courtesy of TrueFire.com (see page 6).

Like making good music, producing a book is a group effort. Big thanks are due the *Guitar Player* writers whose work appears in this second edition of *How to Play Rock Guitar*, as well as to Jesse Gress and Liz Ledgerwood for their music editing/engraving teamwork, Rich Leeds for his design artistry, Greg Isola for his proofreading precision, and Backbeat's Amy Miller for pulling it all together. Thanks also to Brad Wendkos, Alison Hasbach, and everyone else at TrueFire.com for making the online lessons a reality.

—Richard Johnston, Editor

About the Authors

Matt Blackett is a former *Guitar Player* associate editor who has performed and recorded with a number of artists. An audio consultant, he has appeared on television as host of the "Gearhead" segment on *Guitar Kulture*.

Andy Ellis is Editor in Chief of *Frets* magazine and a senior editor for *Guitar Player*. In addition to his performing and studio credits, Andy originated the Sessions instructional series.

Rik Emmett (rikemmett.com) has recorded a number of solo albums since leaving the band Triumph, including the 2002 EMI release *Handiwork*. Rik's Back to Basics column ran in *Guitar Player* for more than ten years.

Dan Erlewine is Director of Technical Operations for Stewart-MacDonald Manufacturing and author of *The Guitar Player Repair Guide* and *How to Make Your Electric Guitar Play Great!* Dan does repair and setup work for many well-known guitarists.

Jim Ferguson is a Grammy-nominated writer, contributor to the *New Grove Dictionary of Jazz*, and former *Guitar Player* staff editor. An accomplished guitarist, Jim offers his instructional works at fergusonguitar.com.

Joe Gore is a guitarist, producer, engineer, and arranger who has worked with artists such as Tom Waits, PJ Harvey, Bijou Phillips, the Eels, and Stella Soleil. Currently a *Guitar Player* contributing editor, he was a *GP* staff editor for more than ten years.

Jesse Gress is the author of *The Guitar Cookbook* and *Guitar Lick Factory*. Jesse tours and records with Todd Rundgren and the Tony Levin Band, and he has served as music editor on several Backbeat titles.

Adam Levy (adamlevy.com) has recorded with artists such as Leni Stern, Trevor Dunn, and Tracy Chapman. His own albums include *Buttermilk Channel* and *With My Guitar and You* (with George Wyle), both on Lost Wax.

Dave Rubin has performed with Chuck Berry, Screamin' Jay Hawkins, and James Brown's JBs. A noted New York guitar teacher, Dave has written a number of instructional books and contributed to *Guitar Player*'s Sessions section.

Notational Symbols

he following symbols are used in *How To Play Rock Guitar* to notate fingerings, techniques, and effects commonly used in guitar music. Certain symbols are found in either the tablature or the standard notation only, not both. For clarity, consult both systems.

4 : Left-hand fingering is designated by small Arabic numerals near note heads (1=first finger, 2=middle finger, 3=third finger, 4=little finger, t=thumb).

p : Right-hand fingering designated by letters (p=thumb, i=first finger, m=middle finger, a=third finger, c=little finger).

② : A circled number (1-6) indicates the string on which a note is to be played.

▬ : Pick downstroke.

V : Pick upstroke.

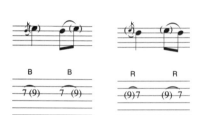

Bend: Play the first note and bend to the pitch of the equivalent fret position shown in parentheses.

Reverse Bend: Pre-bend the note to the specified pitch/fret position shown in parentheses. Play, then release to indicated pitch/fret.

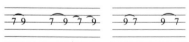

Hammer-on: From lower to higher note(s). Individual notes may also be hammered.

Pull-off: From higher to lower note(s).

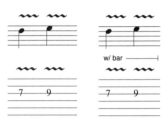

Slide: Play first note and slide up or down to the next pitch. If the notes are tied, pick only the first. If no tie is present, pick both.

A slide symbol before or after a single note indicates a slide to or from an undetermined pitch.

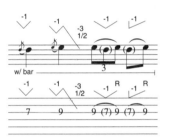

Finger vibrato. Bar vibrato.

Bar dips, dives, and bends: Numerals and fractions indicate distance of bar bends in half-steps.

Natural harmonics. Artificial harmonics.

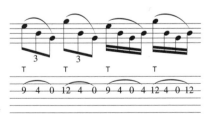

Pick-hand tapping: Notes are hammered with a pick-hand finger, usually followed by additional hammer-ons and pull-offs.

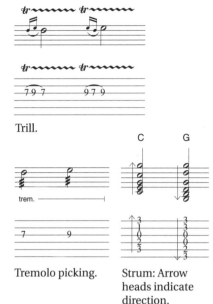

Trill.

Tremolo picking. Strum: Arrow heads indicate direction.

HOW TABLATURE WORKS

The horizontal lines represent the guitar's strings, the top line standing for the high *E*. The numbers designate the frets to be played. For instance, a 2 positioned on the first line would mean play the 2nd fret on the first string (0 indicates an open string). Time values are indicated on the standard notation staff seen directly above the tablature. Special symbols and instructions appear between the standard and tablature staves.

CHORD DIAGRAMS

In all chord diagrams, vertical lines represent the strings, and horizontal lines represent the frets. The following symbols are used:

▬▬▬▬ Nut; indicates first position.

X   Muted string, or string not played.

○   Open string.

⌢   Barre (partial or full).

●   Placement of left-hand fingers.

III Roman numerals indicate the fret at which a chord is located.

Arabic numerals indicate left-hand fingering.

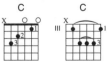

Using the Online Lessons

Backbeat Books and TrueFire have teamed to bring you free audio versions of the lessons in *How to Play Rock Guitar*. Performed and explained by our featured authors as well as noted guitarists such as Brad Carlton, these audio lessons are available at a special Web page created exclusively for *How to Play Rock Guitar*. TrueFire makes it easy for you to access the audio. First, open up the card in the back of this book to claim your unique certificate number—it's your key to all the audio lessons. Next, log on to **PlayRock.TrueFire.com** and, using your certificate number, follow the instructions to register and access the lessons. (The logo below indicates which printed lessons include online audio.) You'll receive a complete set of audio files in a folder you can then download to your own computer. In addition, you'll receive via e-mail a separate certificate number that's worth $10 in TrueFire Cash. You can use this to purchase any of the hundreds of great audio lessons at TrueFire.com, including many by the teachers in *How to Play Rock Guitar*.

Eddie Van Halen

MY TIPS FOR BEGINNERS

BY JIM FERGUSON

Rock guitar god Eddie Van Halen gave Jim Ferguson these timeless tips in the July 1984 Guitar Player.

Rock 'n' roll is feeling. After you know most of the basics—chords, scales, and bends, which we'll discuss here—getting that feeling is just about the most important aspect of playing guitar.

You can't learn to play rock 'n' roll by taking lessons. Although a teacher can show you things like songs and licks, you still have to listen to the music to find out how it feels. My biggest influence was Eric Clapton when he was with Cream and John Mayall's Bluesbreakers. I learned his Cream solos from "Crossroads" (*Wheels of Fire*) and "Sitting on Top of the World" (*Goodbye*) note-for-note by slowing them down to 16 RPM on my dad's record turntable. By taking licks off records and listening, I developed a feel for rock 'n' roll. You'll have to do the same kind of thing. Eventually, you'll take the phrases and rhythm patterns you've copped and begin to put your own mark on them.

Too many guitarists think a player's sound has to do with equipment, but it doesn't make any difference. Once when Van Halen was on tour opening for Ted Nugent, he

was watching me play and wondering how I did it. The next day at the soundcheck he asked our roadie if he could plug into my stuff. Of course, it still sounded like Ted. So it doesn't really matter what you're playing through. Your sound is in your fingers and brain.

If you're going to learn to play lead, get an electric guitar. It doesn't have to be an expensive one (I started on a cheapie Teisco Del Rey). Acoustic guitars aren't good for learning lead, because you can't play up high on the neck, and their heavier-gauge strings make it hard to bend notes. (I use light Fender XL strings.) Also, you don't really need an amp at first, unless you're in a band. When I'm noodling around the house, I rarely plug in.

Ex. 1

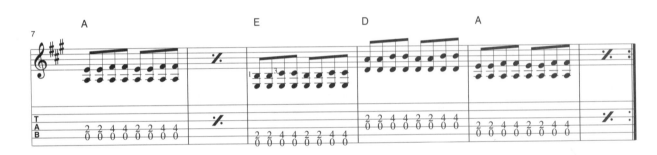

Ex. 2

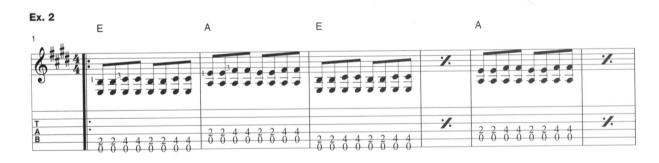

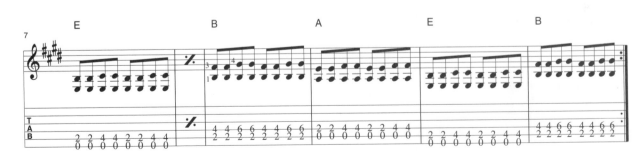

Most beginners want to learn lead because they think it's cool. Consequently, they never really develop good rhythm skills. Since most of a rock guitarist's time is spent playing rhythm, it's important to learn to do it well. Learning lead should come after you can play solid back-up and have the sound of the chords in your head.

Playing blues progressions is the best place to start learning, because they're so basic and they form the foundation for a lot of rock tunes. After you get one or two patterns down in a couple of keys, you can start noodling with lead guitar. **Ex. 1** and **Ex. 2** are shuffle patterns in the keys of *A* and *E* respectively. Memorize them as soon as possible. Eventually you'll want to learn them in other common rock keys, such as *C*, *D*, and *G*. "Ice Cream Man," from our first album, and "Blues Breaker," which I did on Brian May's *Star Fleet Project*, are 12-bar blues.

I learned my first chords from a beginning guitar book that showed the usual *C*, *D*, *D7*, and *Em* down at the nut. But I rarely play chords like that. Listen to the difference between the regular *C* chord and the one that follows it (**Ex. 3**), which sounds much more rock 'n' roll. For a *G* chord I use this fingering (**Ex. 4**) (slightly muffle the bass notes with the heel of your right hand)

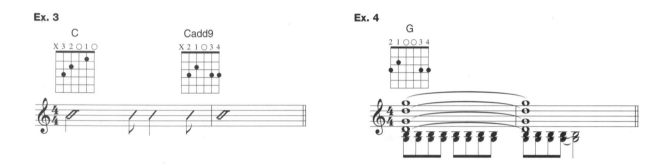

Ex. 3

Ex. 4

A lot of rock players mainly use barre chords, which employ the left-hand 1st finger to cover all six strings at a particular fret, but I usually just two-note it, like the beginning of "On Fire" from *Van Halen* (**Ex. 5**). If you examine the first chord position in Ex. 1, you'll see it's exactly the same as the two-note position here, except moved to the 12th fret and with no open strings.

Ex. 5

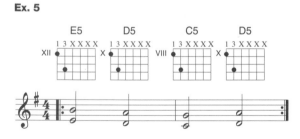

You can make rhythm patterns more interesting by incorporating different riffs. **Ex. 6** illustrates this. It's similar to what I do in "Ain't Talkin' 'Bout Love," also from *Van Halen*. It features a simple bass hook; try using all downstrokes for the two-note parts (more on right-hand picking in a moment). Later in "Ain't Talkin' 'Bout Love" I play the same chords in an arpeggio style. This is another good way to keep things from getting boring (**Ex. 7**).

Ex. 6

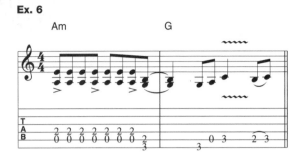

Ex. 7

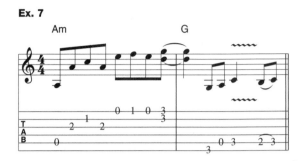

Before we start working on playing lead, I want to talk about right-hand picking. Guys have pointed out that I hold my pick in two ways: with my thumb and middle finger (**Fig. 1**), and with my thumb, index, and middle (**Fig. 2**).

Fig. 1

Fig. 2

Remember that most players don't pick the way I do, so what works for me might not work for you. The important thing is to alternate your picking direction: down, up, down, up, etc. (**Ex. 8**). This method really increases the efficiency of your picking hand. Once you get used to alternating strokes, you'll be able to pick without having to think about it.

The following position for the blues scale is the one most often used by blues and rock players (**Ex. 9**). This scale fits many chords, including the entire 12-bar progression. If you already know this position but still can't play lead very well, then you haven't worked with it enough. (See Rik Emmett's Power of Five, page 15.) Once you learn some hammer-ons, pull-offs, slides, and bends, and how they're incorporated into licks, you'll see why the position is so common (be sure to use alternate picking).

Ex. 8

Ex. 9

The next two patterns are the same as the one we just looked at, only in different locations (**Ex. 10**, **Ex. 11**). Knowing several patterns enables you to play over the entire length of the fingerboard. Also, different positions lend themselves to different licks.

Ex. 10   **Ex. 11**

Another common scale position is the following long form, which spans the 3rd to the 12th fret (**Ex. 12**). Note that when it descends, some of the notes are played on different strings; however, you can go backward through the ascending pattern. (If you do, use your 1st finger to shift downward.) Notice that when you go up, you use the 3rd finger to get to each new position. Also, the area around the 7th fret can produce some especially nice phrases.

Ex. 12

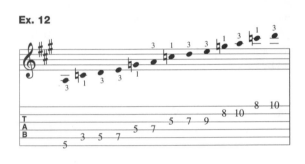

Once you have these scale patterns memorized, it's time to learn how to move them to other keys. For instance, the first pattern becomes an *E* scale when you move it to the 12th fret. You can easily figure this out by moving the root of the scale up the fingerboard chromatically. (The *root* is the note that has the same name as the scale; *chromatically* means by half-steps, or one fret at a time.) For example, on the sixth string the note at the 5th fret is an *A*; at the 6th fret it's an *A♯* (or a *B♭*—they're the same); at the 7th fret it's a *B*, and so on until you get to the 12th fret.

Here's the complete chromatic scale so you can move other patterns on your own. When you get to the end of the scale, *G♯*, continue ascending by starting over at *A*. As long as you know the name of the scale or chord you're starting with, you can move up or down through the chromatic scale; each letter represents one fret (don't use open strings):

A   A♯(B♭)   B   C   C♯(D♭)   D   D♯(E♭)   E   F   F♯(G♭)   G   G♯(A♭)

Knowing note locations is just the beginning. The next step is to start learning the building blocks of licks: hammer-ons, pull-offs, bends, and slides. Hammer-ons and pull-offs can give your notes fluidity and speed. The following phrases are a few short examples for the scale position at the 5th fret (**Examples 13–16**). From here it's your responsibility to transfer the techniques to other phrases and positions.

Ex. 13   **Ex. 14**

Ex. 15   **Ex. 16**

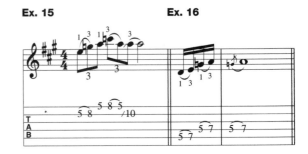

Bending is the technique most often associated with blues and rock soloing, and for that reason it's the most important one to learn. If you're a beginner, there are a couple of things to watch out for. First, don't overshoot the bend; that is, don't bend a note beyond where you intend to go. And once a note is bent, be careful not to use too much finger vibrato (a singing effect produced by rapidly wiggling a string with a fretting-hand finger right after it's been played). If your vibrato wavers too much, you'll overshoot the bend and it'll sound weird.

Here's an exercise for developing bending accuracy (**Ex. 17**). If you can bend with the left-hand pinky, fine, but most players use the 3rd finger because it's stronger. The other fingers can support the one doing the bending. Most bends in rock and blues go up one whole-step; get the correct note in your head by playing the *A* on the second string, 10th fret. Practice bending right up to the *A*. If you hold the note for a while, use slight vibrato.

Now let's learn the bend in combination with some other notes (**Ex. 18**, **Ex. 19**). (A bend *starts* with a bent note, and then releases it.)

Ex. 17   **Ex. 18**   **Ex. 19**

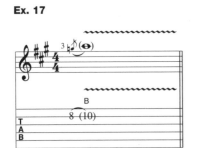
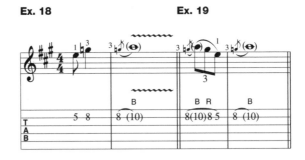

Lots of guys ask which notes I like to bend the most, and I always say all of them. And that's true, depending on the song I'm playing. However, you usually bend some notes more than others. The previous examples use one of the most commonly bent notes. Remember its position in relation to the scale pattern at the 5th fret—it's on the second string and played with the 3rd finger—so you can use it in other keys. Two other good notes to bend, also played with the 3rd finger, are located on the third string, 7th fret (**Fig. 3**) and first string, 8th fret (*C*).

Fig. 3

Here are some licks using both notes, combining them with hammer-ons, pull-offs, and slides (**Examples 20–23**). Practice them until they become second nature, and then find their locations in the other scale patterns. Once things feel comfortable, work on playing lead in different keys and with a variety of rhythms.

Ex. 20   **Ex. 21**   **Ex. 22**   **Ex. 23**

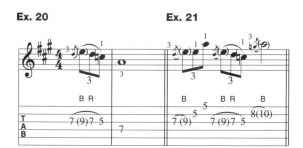   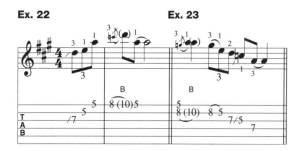

Sometimes I think of new techniques or licks at the strangest times. When I got the idea for right-hand tapping, I was in the bathroom with my guitar. This technique is often written incorrectly in books and played wrong, so here's how it works. To understand the idea, first play this trill with your left hand (**Ex. 24**).

Now tap a finger of your right hand—I usually use the 1st or 2nd finger—to produce the first note, and then pull it off of the string to sound the second (**Fig. 4, Ex. 25**). The pull-off motion should be toward you, and should slightly catch the string. Whole descending scales can be played in this way; try it with the first blues pattern we discussed.

Fig. 4

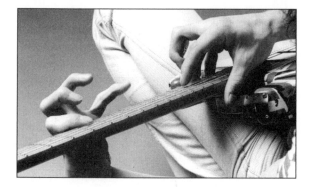

Ex. 24   **Ex. 25**

   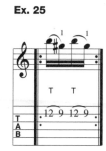

Once you understand the basic moves of tapping (sounding the note with your right hand and pulling off), then you're ready to apply it to a lick. Here's a thing I do in the last part of "Eruption," from *Van Halen* (**Ex. 26**). It's really easy, and makes a great exercise. (You can also play it on the third string.) Notice that after you tap and pull off, you then hammer down to get the third note. When you experiment enough with this technique you'll realize you can get many other combinations.

Ex. 26

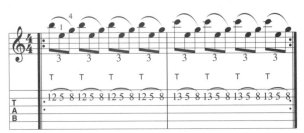

Another easy right-hand technique is harmonic tapping. Examples of this can be heard on "Spanish Fly" and "Women in Love" (*Van Halen II*), "Eruption," and "Top Jimmy" (*1984*). In order to produce a harmonic, just tap 12 frets above a note, directly on the fret—remove your picking-hand finger quickly. Although you can do this technique on an acoustic instrument, you'll get better results on an electric (**Fig. 5**; **Ex. 27**).

Fig. 5

Ex. 27

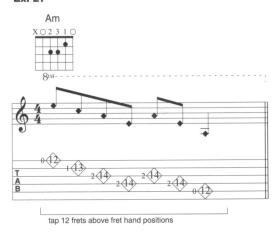

tap 12 frets above fret hand positions

Now that you know some of the basic ingredients of rock 'n' roll, remember that your playing has to have feeling and taste. The goal is to make music, not to just play machine-gun-type stuff. Music is entertainment. You shouldn't be playing it to save the world or show people how great you are. It's just supposed to make you happy, make you cry, or whatever. If it doesn't do that, then it's not music. And remember: You learn by making mistakes. Don't be afraid to try something new. If I'm thrown into an unfamiliar situation, such as playing with a scary guitarist like Allan Holdsworth, I don't panic. Sometimes I skin my knees, but most of the time I land on my feet. My dad has a Dutch saying that puts it much better than I can. Translated, it means, "Ride your bicycle straight through." If you screw up, just keep going. ■

Ian Brown

The Power of Five

GETTING A GRIP
ON PENTATONICS

BY RIK EMMETT

Everybody has music that's a landmark in the soundtrack of their lives. One of mine is the debut album *Led Zeppelin*. When I rediscovered it on CD, it conjured up powerful memories of 1969, when I was a 16-year-old basement-band guitarist. There I was, in my boyhood bedroom, my trusty single-pickup Kay in hand. I was wearing out the needle on the old Seabreeze record player, trying to decipher the beautiful, cascading run that Jimmy Page plays on "Communication Breakdown," when the proverbial light bulb went on over my head. "Hey, that cool pattern he plays over *E* major is the same one I'd use if I were playing blues in the key of *C♯*! I had discovered the beautiful duplicity of the pentatonic scale. If I went three frets below wherever I was playing the basic blues scale pattern, the same fingering yielded a majorish "country" sound.

A pentatonic scale (from the Greek *penta*, meaning five) consists of five notes within each octave. The folk music of many cultures is based on pentatonic scales. ("Auld Lang Syne," for example, has a pentatonic melody.) We usually encounter pentatonic scales in one of two contexts: The first is a *major pentatonic scale*, with the root plus scale degrees 2, 3, 5, and 6. You can think of it as a major scale that's "missing" scale degrees 4 and 7 (**Ex. 1**). The second is a *minor pentatonic* or *blues* scale, with the root plus ♭3, 4, 5, and ♭7 (**Ex. 2**). The ♭3 and ♭7 of the blues pentatonic scale are the legendary "blue notes."

Ex. 1

E major

root 2 3 4 5 6 7 (1)

E major pentatonic

root 2 3 5 6 (1)

Ex. 2

E minor "blues" pentatonic

root ♭3 4 5 ♭7 (root)

Here's my Party Trick No. 278: Drag your fingers harp-style across a piano's black keys while holding down the sustain pedal. Not only will everyone be impressed that you've been so modestly concealing your keyboard skills, but you'll have played a G♭ major pentatonic scale (or an E♭ blues scale—remember E♭ is three frets below G♭).

Each pentatonic fingering can be interpreted as either major or blues/minor, depending on which note you designate as the root. **Ex. 3** shows major and minor pentatonic scale fingerings (for *E* major and *C♯* blues respectively) in five positions. Notice that the fingerings are the same for both scale types, but that different notes serve as the root.

The two pentatonic scales are not mutually exclusive. Our culture's pop music has assimilated both, so you can combine them in the same song, solo, or even in the same bar of a riff. Try playing over a 12-bar blues progression using the blues/minor pentatonic fingerings. Then, try sliding any of the five fingerings down three frets to get the major "country" sound. Get-

Ex. 3

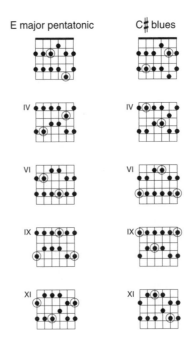

E major pentatonic   C♯ blues

ting a grasp of this concept is a good first step toward understanding the more advanced modal superimposition concepts of jazz/fusion players such as Frank Gambale and Larry Carlton.

A word about the power of the number 5: The 5th is the most basic, powerful interval, and the circle of 5ths is a fundamental concept in music theory. (The ancient Chinese revered the number 5 because it signified the five elements, the five types of human relationships, and the five types of grain.) In our microtonal, polychromatic world, the pentatonic scale is a profound, primal means of expression that we still may not appreciate or understand fully enough.

THE FIVE-BLOCK SYSTEM

Let's examine one of the most important concepts for understanding the fingerboard: the block system. In the July 1984 *Guitar Player*, Jim Ferguson wrote Scale Systems, a column I've recommended often. It introduces readers to the classic five-block system, which is based on five simple first-position chord forms (**Ex. 4**).

Ex. 4

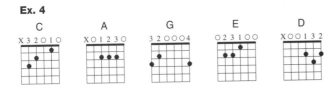

Now let's take the five forms and put them on the fingerboard as different voicings of the same chord, in the same key, all the way up the neck (**Ex. 5**). Don't get confused—the chords at the top of Ex. 5 are all *C* chords, but they're labeled according to the visual shape of the first-position chords. The diatonic major scales that correspond to each chord form are shown at the bottom of the example. The root notes—all *C*'s in this case—are circled. You should photocopy Ex. 5 and tack it up in your practice area. It's probably the most important building block of fretboard knowledge.

Ex. 5

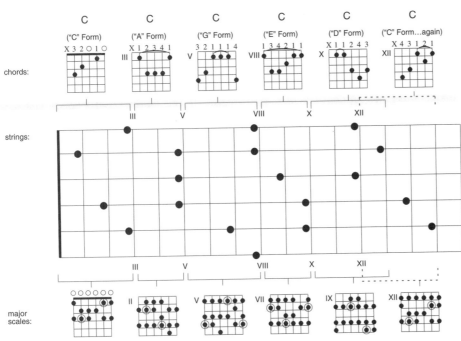

Now you've got a system that covers the entire fingerboard. Your challenge is to transpose it into all the major keys. After 30,000 fretboard miles, you should be able to do it stone cold.

THE FIVE W'S

Once you've figured out the five-block major scale patterns in all keys, you can double-check your work against **Ex. 6** and **Ex. 7**. Those of you who claim that the dog ate your homework should feel ashamed—consider these offerings a free introductory gift. Come up with fingerings for the other nine keys on your own, and say three "Hail Chuck Berrys" as penance for your indolence.

Ex. 6

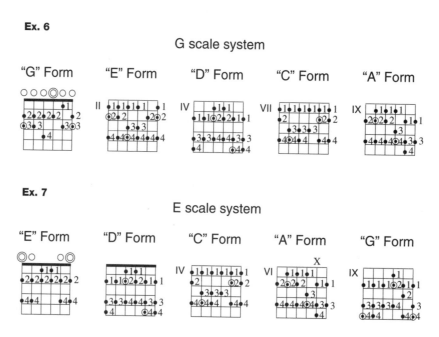

To fully assimilate the five-block system into your playing, you must connect the dots. How will you shift from one scale position to the next? **Ex. 8** shows one way to combine three positions in order to execute a smooth run. In the ascending run, the first five notes come from the "E-form" G scale. The arrow represents a shift up to the "D-form" G scale for the next seven notes. A second shift takes you up to the "C-form" G scale for the final six notes.

When and where to shift is a matter of personal choice—comfort and ease of memorization are the most important criteria. (But this doesn't mean that you don't have to work it out!)

Ex. 8

Before signing off on the topic of five, here's one more thing to chew on: Journalists are taught to address the five W's: Who, What, When, Where, and Why. Musicians should ask themselves the same questions.

Who? Have I committed my heart and soul to the music? Who is my audience, and am I reaching them?

What? Do I understand what I'm doing? Do I have perspective and awareness? What is the significance of the music to me and my audience?

When? Timing is everything. Is my playing appropriate? Am I playing the right note at the right time? Am I adding to the groove? Can I give the performance a real sense of occasion?

Where? "Where" is closely related to "when." I once saw Larry Carlton and B.B. King together on a TV show. Larry said that when he wanted to improve his phrasing and placement, he went back to B.B.'s records and found that he was playing everywhere that B.B. wasn't and vice versa. He turned his playing around, and the rest is history.

Why? A good actor searches for motivation. If you want to make it really matter, you've got to have a reason. You don't necessarily have to spell it out for your audience, but if you know why you're playing something, they'll know the difference. ■

Pull Out the Stops

INCREASE YOUR CHORD VOCABULARY WITH DOUBLE- & TRIPLE-STOPS

BY DAVE RUBIN

DOUBLE-STOPS

Like Little Richard, who once proclaimed himself both the king and queen of rock 'n' roll, double-stops have dual distinctions: They can function as chordal indicators or harmonized solos, or both.

Double-stops are classified according to the interval between the low and high note. Let's check out double-stops in 6ths. (3rds, 4ths, and 5ths are other common intervals found in most forms of music.) In pop music, most double-stops are derived from the Ionian (major), Aeolian (natural minor), and Mixolydian (dominant) modes. **Ex. 1** harmonizes the G Mixolydian mode (1, 2, 3, 4, 5, 6, ♭7 = G, A, B, C, D, E, F) on the first and third strings; **Ex. 2** transfers the same idea to the second and fourth strings. I've notated the scales horizontally over the span of an octave, though they can also be played in a single position across shifting pairs of strings.

Ex. 1

Ex. 2

Ex. 3 contains the classic "sliding 9th" lick found in blues standards like "Stormy Monday." It's constructed from the *G* and *C* Mixolydian modes (bars 1 and 2, respectively). This is totally cool as a lead/rhythm part against a guitar or keyboard banging out triplet chords over a slow 12/8 groove.

Chuck Berry's "Memphis" is based on the sliding pattern in **Ex. 4**. The effect is that of a major chord (suggested by scale degrees 1 and 3, *G* and *B*) shifting to a dominant chord ($\flat$7 and 9, *F* and *A*). For a real greasy I–IV–V progression, shift the lick to the IV and V chords (*C* at the 8th fret and *D* at the 10th fret).

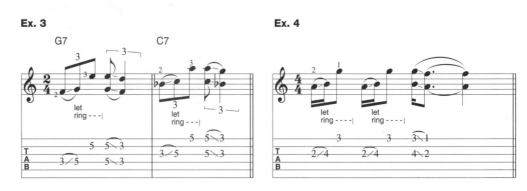

Ex. 5 uses the kind of garden-variety double-stops found in the intro hook of Van Morrison's "Brown-Eyed Girl." Bar 2 implies the IV chord (*C*) and can be seen as the first three degrees of a harmonized *C* Mixolydian mode, or as the 4th, 5th, and 6th degrees of *G* Mixolydian. As you can see, the Mixolydian mode is a helpful tool for covering I–IV changes. Bluesman Robert Johnson's signature dominant/diminished chord turnaround can be reduced to the double-stop sequence in **Ex. 6**. Note that a passing interval (*B$\flat$/D$\flat$*) has been inserted between the 2nd and 3rd degrees of the *G* Mixolydian mode. This implied diminished chord ensures a smooth transition to the root triad.

Theoretically speaking, chords need at least three notes to be fully defined. But we can substitute double-stops for chords if we carefully match the key signatures. Remember, when you are conscious of the proper changes, you will always be harmonically—if not politically—correct.

TRIPLE-STOPS

Three-note chord forms were extensively employed by rock guitarists even before '60s British bands like the Kinks began overdriving their Vox AC30 amps. Amid the current disarray of grunge, punk-funk, rap-rock, and pop bands, it seems prudent for the thinking guitarist to rise above the morass by expanding his or her chordal vocabulary with triple-stops, which are groups of three simultaneous notes.

Triple-stops are often triads. The most common triads are major (1, 3, 5), minor (1, ♭3, 5), augmented (1, 3, ♯5), and diminished (1, ♭3, ♭5). The following chart shows these forms with the root note of C:

Major	Minor	Augmented	Diminished
1–3–5	1–♭3–5	1–3–♯5	1–♭3–♭5
C–E–G	C–E♭–G	C–E–G♯	C–E♭–G♭

Dominant chords—7s, 9s, 13s, and the like—theoretically require at least four notes, but they can often be implied with triple-stops. **Ex. 1** shows the A major scale harmonized in triads. Memorize these useful forms in all the major keys. The diagonal lines in the chord names indicate that these are inversions; their lowest notes are not their roots. Such inversions are sometimes called "slash chords" (no, not that Slash, thank you). Please note that chord number seven in the series, G♯m♭5, has the same shape as Ex. 4's rootless dominant 7 chord. Context is all-important when identifying three-note chords.

Ex. 1

Ex. 2 shows the root position and first and second inversions of an A major triad. This series sounds slick as a substitute for a single chord. **Ex. 3** shows the corresponding A minor and inversions. If you go back to Ex. 1 and work out the root positions and inversions for each triad, you'll probably get a headache. You will also have enough chord forms ready to express yourself with more vim and verve. **Ex. 4** lacks the root A, but it can function as A7, especially if another instrument supplies the missing tonic.

Ex. 2 **Ex. 3** **Ex. 4**

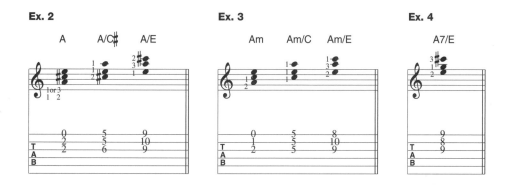

Lots of classic blues and rock tunes feature three-note chords. **Ex. 5** is based on a theme that appears in the Electric Flag's version of "Killing Floor." The Bobby Fuller Four's "I Fought the Law" and Buddy Holly's "Peggy Sue" both use patterns similar to **Ex. 6**.

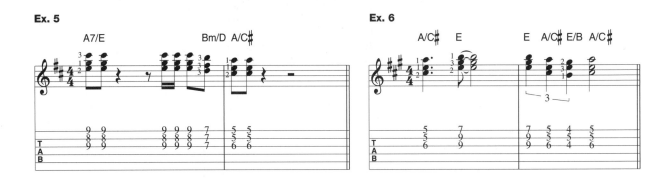

Ex. 7 shows how triadic inversions can help connect a chord progression. Notice how the melody notes on the high *E* string descend chromatically from *A* to *E*—hip stuff! Both the Eagles' "Hotel California" and the Rolling Stones' "Wild Horses" can be arranged in this manner. ∎

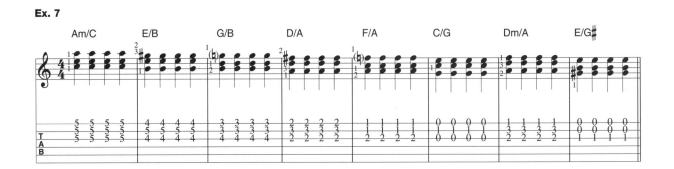

Wah-Wah User's Guide

A LESSON FROM THE MASTERS

BY JOE GORE

Nothing reveals inexperienced wah wankers so readily as their tendency to simply rock the pedal on the beat. No shame in that—most of us have a hard enough time just playing with two hands without having to bring a third limb into the equation. Tapping a foot in time to the music is probably the safest way to begin.

The true wizards of wah approach the pedal much less predictably. They sculpt each note to best suit the musical context, which requires a level of hand/foot coordination that may seem elusive at first. Consider the famous riff from the Jimi Hendrix *Electric Ladyland* classic "Voodoo Chile (Slight Return)." **Ex. 1** shows a lick in the style

Ex. 1

of the passage that commences about 10 seconds into the song. The wah notation—"o" for "open" (maximum treble) position and, later in this lesson, a circled "x" for "closed" (minimum treble) position—is admittedly crude. It doesn't take into account the spectrum of sounds available between the two extreme settings. But even so, we can see how free and funky Jimi's accents are.

Since the "open" position is the wah's loudest sound, notes played in that way stand out in relation to their neighbors (*duh!*—but bear with me). In the first four bars, the wah accents tend to fall on the offbeat eighth-notes (the "and" of each beat), implying a subtle double-time backbeat feel, almost as if a snare drum were hitting there. The drums enter at the end of bar 4, at which point Jimi turns the feel around, placing most of the accents on the downbeats along with Mitch Mitchell's bass drum. Too tough.

How can you cultivate that sort of rhythmic unpredictability, the independence of motion that lets your hands and feet perform different tasks simultaneously? Take a clue from drummers, who often devote huge amounts of energy to cultivating the kinetic independence of each limb. C'mon—if *drummers* can do it, you certainly can.

Ex. 2a is probably the next easiest thing to tapping the wah on the beat. Offbeat wah rhythms are most readily playable when the foot motion doubles a corresponding hand motion. Here you depress the wah into open/treble position for the riff's highest notes. (The crescendo/decrescendo wedges indicate the opening and closing of the pedal.) Again, we're

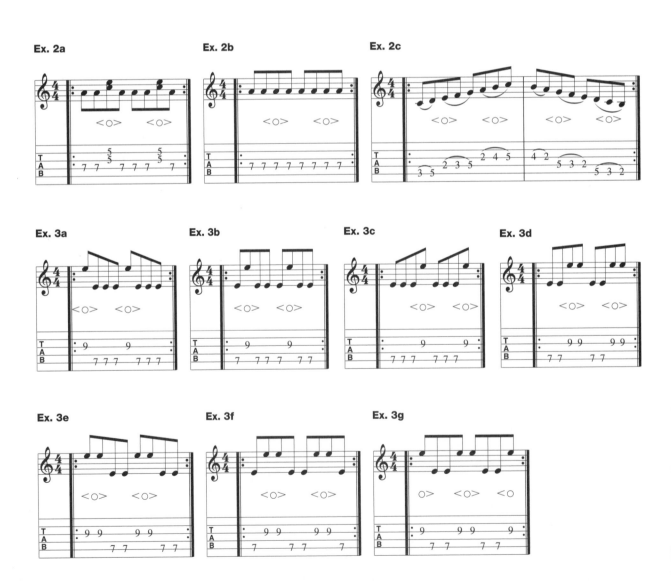

implying a snare-like backbeat feel. After you can play Ex. 2a comfortably with a metronome at a medium rock tempo—120 BPM, say—try **Ex. 2b**. It's the same wah pattern, but set against a single note. Your foot is no longer cued by the motion of your hands.

Next, try maintaining the wah pattern against a melodic figure that doesn't correspond to the foot pattern—a major or pentatonic scale, for example. As you become more confident, try patterns like **Ex. 2c**, in which the hand motions—pick strokes, melodic contour, placement of string changes and slurs—occur completely independently of the wah accents.

Examples 3a through **3g** show other rhythmic patterns you can subject to the same three-step process we used in Ex. 2. Try each figure first using a high note to mark the wah accent, as notated; next, try it on just a single note; finally, try superimposing the wah pattern over different melodies. Change the notes (those octave E's get old real fast) or work with double-stops and full chords. Contrast clean, clearly articulated notes with percussive scratching. And after you can play these at about 140 BPM or more, halve the tempo and try the examples with a 16th-note funk feel.

So far, our examples have focused on fast opening and closing of the wah filter. But long sweeps are equally cool. A gradual opening and closing can flavor an extended solo—just ask Metallica's Kirk Hammett—or impart a funky, analog synth–like filter envelope to a short, repetitious figure. **Ex. 4** evokes an early-'70s wah style exemplified by the guitar part on Isaac Hayes' "Theme from *Shaft*." The wah opens slowly, but there is a clear dynamic accent on the fourth beat of each measure. "Tracking" the melodic contour of a long line (**Ex. 5**) is also effective.

Ex. 4

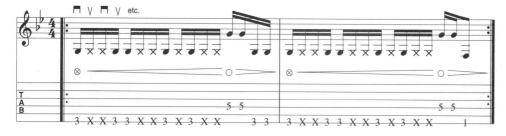

Ex. 5

Another trippy sound is a rapid flutter, most effective against sustained chords. Eric Clapton uses this device to good effect on the bridge of Cream's "White Room," from *Wheels of Fire*. To cop the style, check **Ex. 6**. Clapton's wah timing seems deliberately irregular, but you can perfect this difficult technique by practicing wah pulses in steady eighth-notes, eighth-note triplets, and 16th-notes against a metronome pulse. When timed, the effect sounds like exaggerated amp tremolo. Try approximating the overstated tremolo effect on Tommy James & the Shondells' '60s bubblegum fave "Crimson and Clover" by wiggling the wah in regular 16th-notes over a I–V–IV–V progression such as *G–D–C–D*.

Ex. 6

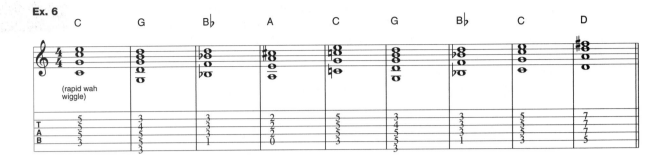

Swelling into each note is a relatively easy move that you can practice with any melody. But just for fun, try wahing into each of the descending tritones in **Ex. 7**, a yuk-yuk signifier you've heard in cartoon soundtracks. Attacking a note with the wah in maximum open/treble position and then quickly "gulping" down into closed position is a bit trickier; it sounds good paired with quick descending slides like those in **Ex. 8**.

Ex. 7   **Ex. 8**

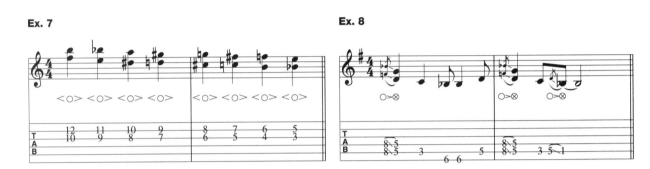

Ex. 8 touches on one of the most fascinating aspects of wah playing: the *relationship* between tone (as determined by the wah) and pitch. The bluesy licks in **Ex. 9** develop this idea a bit more. Notes that are bent upward are paired with opening of the wah, reverse bends with closing. Psychoacoustically speaking, we seem to want to correlate brightness of tone with highness of pitch. Try experimenting with the opposite arrangement by reversing the wah moves in Ex. 9. It may feel strange, but you may find some great possibilities there.

Ex. 9

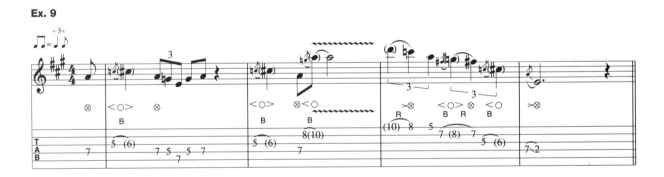

To see how perfectly pitch, tone, articulation, and timbre can interact, let's turn to the work of the players I consider to be wah's supreme wonder workers: not guitarists, but the horn geniuses of Duke Ellington's '20s and '30s bands. Trumpeters Bubber Miley and Cootie Williams and trombonist Tricky Sam Nanton created sublime wah effects by working rubber plunger caps against the bells of their horns. Their wah inflections, lip slurs, glissandos, and "growl" effects mesh in endlessly subtle and varied ways. **Ex. 10** is a crude approximation of the sort of blues licks Miley played on Ellington's 1920s recordings of "East St. Louis Toodle-Oo." (You can hear versions on collections such as *The Best of Early Ellington*, GPR; *Ellington in the Twenties*, EPM; and *Ken Burns Jazz: Duke Ellington*, Sony/Columbia.)

Note how Miley uses devices rarely attempted by guitarists, such as rapidly alternating "open" and "closed" versions of the same pitch (an effect we can heighten by playing the pitch on different strings, as in bar 6). Also note the great variation in the rate of wah application—everything from instant back-and-forth to gradual swells. There's never a false move, and certainly none of the nervous fidgeting you hear from less-than-experienced wah-wrangling six-stringers. Remember, too, that our crude notation doesn't capture the gradations between the full-open and full-closed positions. ∎

Ex. 10

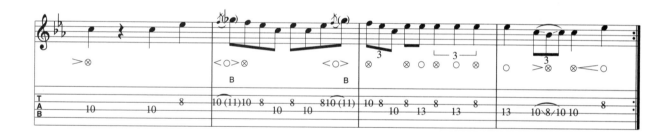

Scotty Moore with Elvis Presley, 1956

© Michael Ochs Archives.com

Roots Rock Pilgrimage

REVISIT THE PIONEERING RIFFS OF SCOTTY MOORE & CARL PERKINS

BY ANDY ELLIS

The ruckus we call rock 'n' roll began in a storefront studio at 706 Union Avenue, in Memphis, Tennessee. Bored with the big-band music of the day, engineer and radio announcer Sam Phillips started Memphis Recording Service in 1950 "to make records with some of the great Negro artists" he'd heard perform locally. Ike Turner, B.B. King, and Howlin' Wolf made their first records at Memphis Recording Service, and while their blues mojo was the real deal, Phillips knew most white

Slapback!

As Brian Setzer says, "You've got to have a slap on there for a rockabilly sound." While it's hard to pinpoint who was the first to use slap echo, the jittery sound was immortalized by Sam Phillips and Sun Records artists in the early '50s. Originally, slap echo was produced in the studio by using a second reel-to-reel tape machine to produce the signal delay, but you can cop the vibe using today's digital delays.

Start by setting the delay time. Slapback echo spans a range of about 50 to 500 milliseconds (a half second). Settings from 50ms to 100ms create a quick jolt, and you'll hear a distinct repeat at settings above 125ms. The key is to experiment until you find a setting that sits well with the song's tempo.

For an authentic Sun Records stutter, you want a single echo—which means setting your delay repeat knob (also called feedback or regeneration) to 0. Using the mix control, make the echo prominent, yet not quite as loud as the original signal. Finally, to better emulate a tape machine, roll off the echo's high end. The original note should sparkle and the slap should sound a bit wooly. Some digital delays—such as Line 6's DL4 Delay Modeler—let you go one step further by adding a hint of pitch wobble (to simulate a tape deck's inherent wow and flutter) and distortion (to suggest tape saturation).

teenagers weren't ready for such uncompromising sounds. The wily producer desperately wanted to find a hillbilly singer who could reflect some African-American heat and cash in on the massive—but yet untapped—crossover potential. His prayers were answered in July 1954, when a nervous 19-year-old named Elvis Presley showed up to audition for Phillips' fledgling Sun Records.

Phillips drafted two studio pros—electric guitarist Scotty Moore and upright bassist Bill Black—to accompany Presley's jangling acoustic guitar for the audition. When the trio launched into an impromptu version of Arthur "Big Boy" Crudup's "That's All Right," streetwise blues lyrics collided with a hopped-up country beat, and musical history was irrevocably altered. Moore's syncopated picking and twangy double-stops were a perfect foil for Presley's jumpy vocals. Between July '54 and July '55, Presley and crew recorded some 30 tracks, and, in the process, Moore blazed a trail for a new generation of pickers. As Jeff Beck put it, "The Elvis stuff was the real start of it. That was the rocket ship taking off for a whole bunch of us."

It didn't take long for this "hillbilly blues beat" to conquer the airwaves. But it was songwriter and ace guitarist Carl Perkins—not Presley—who gave Phillips his first million seller. In 1956, a few months after Phillips had sold Presley's Sun Records contract to RCA Victor, Perkins topped the pop, country, *and* R&B charts with "Blue Suede Shoes." A triple-chart hit was unprecedented, and though Perkins's career was derailed by a near-fatal auto accident, he became a rock-guitar pioneer.

In this lesson, we'll explore quick, easy ways to emulate the twitchy vibe that Moore and Perkins unleashed at Sun Records in the mid '50s. You can use these early rockabilly moves in a variety of settings, including up-tempo blues, swampy R&B, and honky-tonk. For an authentic Sun Records sound, you'll need echo, but these licks work equally well without effects.

Moore was a consummate accompanist, and the arpeggiated riffs he draped over Presley's manic flat-top in "That's All Right" helped fill out the music without being intrusive. "I wanted to play something that would complement the song and the singer," said Moore. "That's what people still have such a hard time doing, and that's really all I ever had in mind. Merle Travis and Chet Atkins were my idols, but I couldn't play with my thumb and fingers, or duplicate note-for-note what they were doing. I would take a little phrase—blues, country, whatever—and turn it around to make it fit something I was trying to do. I tried to keep a rhythm going and nose on in with stabs here and there. I wasn't thinking about creating a new style."

Inspired by Moore's cool comping and sense of economy, **Ex. 1a** reveals an essential hillbilly blues trick: Rather than play five- or six-string dominant 7 voicings, pare the harmony down to three notes. Because the dominant 7 formula (1, 3, 5, ♭7) specifies a minimum of four tones, we must selectively drop one note from each voicing. For example, in bar 1, sketch *E7* by juggling the 1, 3, and ♭7 (*E*, *G♯*, and *D*). In bar 2, similarly abbreviate *D7*—only this time, wrangle the 3, 5, and ♭7 (*F♯*, *A*, and *C*). For bar 3's *A7*, again use the 3, 5, and ♭7 (*C♯*, *E*, and *G*), but in a new order.

As you play through this example, scan the melodic movement on each string. Notice how when we shift from *E7* to *D7*, two lines ascend, while one descends. Moving from *D7* to *A7* reverses the process: Two lines descend, while one ascends. Such contrary motion is a byproduct of tight voice-leading.

In **Ex. 1b**, we shift to a lower position and repeat the chord-trimming process using a slightly busier picking pattern. We encountered bar 1's grip in the previous example, but bar 2's *D7* is a new shape consisting of 3, 5, and ♭7 (*F♯*, *A*, and *C*). In rockabilly and swing, it's common to use a major 6 (adding the scale's 6th degree) for the I chord, as we do in bar 3 with *A6* (*A*, *C♯*, *E*, *F♯*).

Ex. 1c borrows grips from Ex. 1a and Ex. 1b to create yet another variation of the V–IV–I cadence.

These three examples are highly concentrated. Once you've grasped the different voicings and picking patterns, try spinning complete 12-bar progressions in the key of *A* using

Ex. 1a

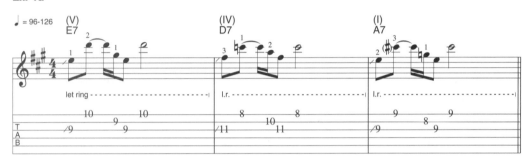

Ex. 1b

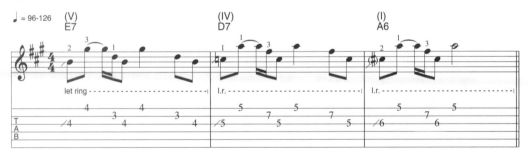

Ex. 1c

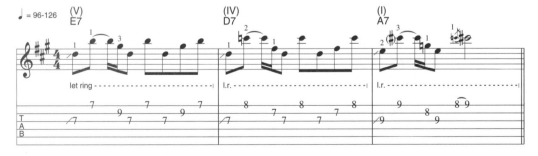

different combinations of the chords and rhythms shown here. Keep it simple—imagine that you're adding harmonic sophistication to a churning acoustic guitar and clicky, slapped upright bass. Observe the "let ring" markings and use a hybrid pick-and-fingers attack—flatpick, middle, and ring fingers on the third, second, and first strings respectively.

We get even more melodic in **Ex. 2**, which dances through a series of dominant 7 and major 6 voicings to create another V–IV–I progression in *A*. Even with this increased activity, the voicings stay compact—we're sketching each chord using only three strings. It's a timeless sound that stretches from Sam Phillips' Sun Records through early Beatles cover tunes, and into such contemporary alt-country heavies as Lucinda Williams.

Ex. 2

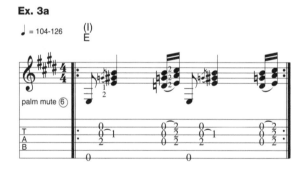

Many early rock classics—including "Mystery Train," which Presley, Moore, and Black cut at Sun Records in '55—feature a chugging train-style rhythm like the one shown in **Ex. 3a**. With a little slapback, it makes an irresistible groove. Play this snappy I–IV move over an *E* or *E7* chord, and remember to palm-mute the sixth string. If you have difficulty nailing this lopsided rhythm, first plunk the open *E* on beats *one* and *three*, then add the chords on the upbeats. Finally, slip in the grace notes.

Ex. 3b shows a movable variation of this rockin' beat. In this version, your thumb frets the root. Again, start simply and then add the embellishments. With a bit of ingenuity, you'll be able to string together Ex. 3a and Ex. 3b to create a full I–IV–V, 12-bar train groove in *E*.

Ex. 3a

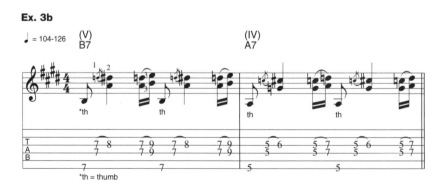

Ex. 3b

When Moore wanted to get really concise, he'd imply dominant 7's using only tritones. (A tritone is an interval of three whole-steps, such as C#–G.) A dominant 7 contains a tritone between the 3 and ♭7, the chord's two most important tones. By playing this interval, you can suggest the full harmony without hogging much sonic space. Here's an *A7* chord spelled out to show where the 3–♭7 tritone lies:

1	<u>3</u>	5	<u>♭7</u>
A	<u>*C#*</u>	*E*	<u>*G*</u>

In September '54, when Presley and crew cut the swinging "Good Rockin' Tonight," Moore used tritones in his horn-like comping and sassy solos. To get a feel for his approach, try **Ex. 4**. If you're having trouble sonically extrapolating each chord from its tritone, briefly play the chord's root before digging into the corresponding tritone figure, and everything will snap into focus. You can play through an entire I–IV–V progression using the tritones shown here. It's a hip and funky sound.

Ex. 4

Moore played **Ex. 5**'s four-bar figure in both of his "Good Rockin' Tonight" solos. Perkins and Roy Orbison—another Sun Records discovery—also used these licks in their recorded solos. Decades later, Stevie Ray Vaughan would turn heads with the same moves.

The phrase begins with rowdy duplicate *E*s. Because the fretted *E* is never perfectly in tune with its open neighbor, you get an edgy, vibrant unison. In bar 2, give the *G* a quarter bend and then hold it against the high *B*. The resulting interval tantalizingly hovers between minor and major.

The clangy interval in bar 4 is the single most important move in '50s lead guitar. This too is a tritone, but it differs from Ex. 4's tritone in two ways: In Ex. 4, we played tritones along the second and third strings, which yielded a warm midrange timbre. This time, the tritone occurs on the first and second strings, and thus has a more cutting tone. Most significant,

Ex. 5

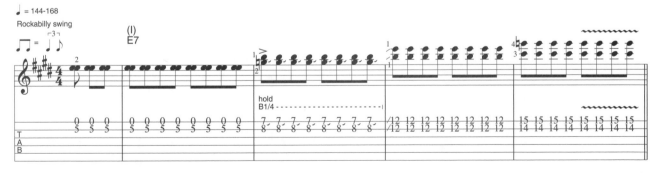

Ex. 5's tritone nails different notes in relation to the underlying harmony. Before, we picked the 3 and ♭7, but here we're hitting the 6 and ♭3—in this instance, *C♯* and *G* against *E7*. For extra attitude, give these notes some fast vibrato in beats *three* and *four*.

Let's work with the 6-♭3 tritone in another context. The next three licks illustrate how to slip it into bluesy phrases in the key of *A*. Record the harmony—or have a friend play the changes—so you can hear the tritone stinging the *A7*.

A I–IV phrase, **Ex. 6a** is derived from Perkins's "Blue Suede Shoes." We begin with the tangy 6-♭3 tritone (*F♯–C*), toy with the ♭5 (*E♭*), stretch the 4 (*D*) slightly while holding the 6 (*F♯*), and finally anticipate the IV (*D9*) by playing its ♭7 and 9 (*C* and *E*). **Ex. 6b** is inspired by figures Perkins played in "Gone, Gone, Gone." The skanky 6–♭3 tritone dominates bar 1, while bar 2's *A6* offers a hint of cowboy swing.

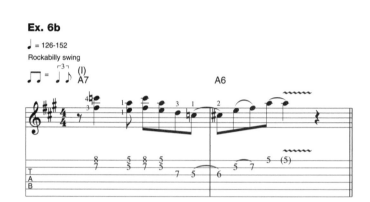

Ex. 6a

Ex. 6b

To play roots rock, you have to have some cool, deep-twangin' bass-string riffs at your fingertips. In December 1954, Presley recorded numerous takes of "I'm Left, You're Right, She's Gone." The alternate takes featured the simple yet soulful line in **Ex. 7a**, played by Moore. Here we're riffing against an *E* chord—jump one string-set higher, and you'll have an *A* riff. Hot dog!

To drive his pulsing "Matchbox," Perkins played the boogie moves in **Ex. 7b**. This was in 1955. Two decades later, Billy Gibbons would rework these ideas for such ZZ Top rockers as "Heard It on the X." See how the threads connect?

Inspired by riffage Perkins played in his '55 smash, "Honey Don't," **Ex. 7c** is an essential bass-string passage. It's a V–I move here, but you can easily build a complete I–IV–V groove

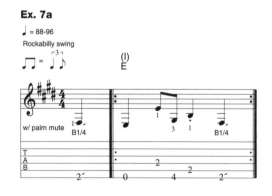

Ex. 7a

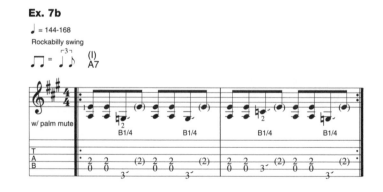

Ex. 7b

from these four measures. To cover *A7* (the IV), simply jump the fingering in bars 3 and 4 up to the fifth and fourth strings. Keep it clean, make it swing, observe the slides, and lay on some hearty slap echo. For variety, try palm muting.

Ex. 7c

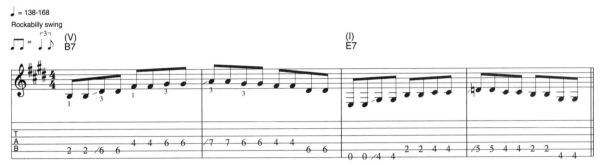

We'll close with a cool tribute to Buddy Holobaugh, who played the wicked guitar licks in Warren Smith's 1956 Sun Records hit, "Rock 'n' Roll Ruby." **Ex. 8** shows how Holobaugh suggests major 6 chords by using relative minor triads.

It works like this: *F#m* (*F#*, *A*, *C#*)—the relative minor of *A*—contains the 6, root, and 3 of an *A6* chord (*A*, *C#*, *E*, *F#*, or 1, 3, 5, 6). It's easier to fret a minor triad than a full major 6 chord, yet you get all the important notes—hip. Just remember this mantra: When you need to play a major 6, try fretting its relative minor triad instead. (You'll find the relative minor lurking three frets below any given major chord.) For *D6*, play *Bm*; for *G6*, play *Em*, and so on. This trick works best when you're playing with another harmonic instrument, and you've got the high part.

In addition to the major 6/relative minor substitution, Holobaugh also makes use of the "cosmic law of chordal chromaticism," which goes something like this: You can engage in any form of chromatic shenanigans if you nail your destination chord from a half-step away at the start of a new measure. "Rock 'n' Roll Ruby" has a standard blues structure, which dictates that the IV (in this instance, *D6*) occurs on bar 5's downbeat. The 12 chordal shifts Smith executes in bars 3 and 4 build tension that gets released in bar 5. Astute readers will notice that in bar 4, beat *four*, the penultimate move is a downward whole-step jump. Hey—like Holobaugh, do whatever it takes to make that final chromatic *Db6–D6* push happen on the new bar's downbeat. ■

Ex. 8

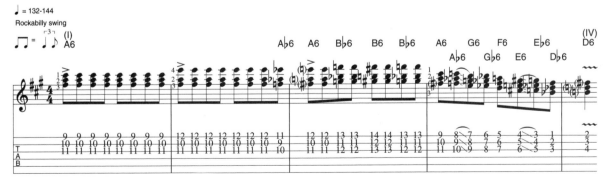

Dick Dale at Ciro's, circa 1963

Hodad No More!

A SURF GUITAR PRIMER

BY JESSE GRESS

Hodad: One who hangs around surf spots, pretending to be a surfer.

The early '60s were make-it-or-break-it years for electric guitar. The instrument dominated rock 'n' roll during the '50s, but by the end of the decade the future was not looking too rosy for our beloved canoe paddles. Between the acoustic purism of the burgeoning folk-music scene and the elaborate orchestrations increasingly favored by pop and rock producers, electric guitars were being pushed into the background. By 1960, even Duane Eddy's pristine twang was smothered in strings. But thanks to a few visionaries and some ingenious marketing, instrumental guitar music and electric guitar sales were booming by 1963. The reason? Surf music.

The surf craze reinstated the electric guitar at pop's forefront—with a vengeance. Learning tunes like the Chantays' "Pipeline" and the Surfaris' "Wipe Out" became a rite of passage for budding rockers, but the key player was surf guitar guru Dick Dale. He and his group, the Del-Tones, virtually defined the genre on such early hits as "Miserlou" and "Surf Beat."

Record companies cashed in on the craze with scores of cheesy instrumental guitar records by fictitious "groups" made up of studio musicians. Established acts also jumped on the bandwagon. While the Ventures' wonderful *Surfin'* album features surf-style originals as well as a cover of "Pipeline," the band wasn't born as and didn't remain strictly a surf outfit. And while the Beach Boys and other vocal groups were certainly influenced by Dale and company, the bulk of authentic surf guitar lies within the repertoires of the Del-Tones, the Chantays, the Surfaris, and lesser-known bands such as the Lively Ones, the Sentinels, the Astronauts (from Boulder, Colorado), Eddie & the Showmen (named after the Fender Showman amp), the Challengers, the Jesters (featuring a young Jim Messina of later "Loggins &" fame), the Avantis, and the Tornadoes. (Rhino's *Guitar Player Presents the Legends of Guitar: Surf Vol. 1* collects gems by such groups, and with its superbly detailed liner notes by instrumental rock authority John Blair, the record makes a perfect starting point for newcomers.)

Gear-wise, Dick Dale set the standard. Fender guitars, especially Strats, Jaguars, and Jazzmasters, were the weapons of choice, though the Ventures endorsed Mosrites. Fender amps were also a big part of the sound; Dale even helped design the high-wattage Dual Showman. Dale, who still kicks serious instrumental-rock ass, plays lefty without reversing his strings, à la Albert King, and Dale still wields the custom gold metal-flake Stratocaster he acquired in the early '60s. Another important element of the surf guitar sound was liberal application of spring reverb, either from free-standing or built-in units.

Before you catch the wave, a few ground rules: Use medium- to heavy-gauge strings, don't bend single notes much more than a half-step, use many open strings, and apply tremolo picking when appropriate (that is, wherever possible). Now crank your reverb to 11, empty your mind, and become one with this drum beat:

The Duane Eddy–style tremolo-bar dips in **Ex. 1a** served as the intro to many a surf tune. Manipulate the bar with either hand. You can transpose the lick to the open *A* string to imply a change to the IV chord, and then to the fifth-string, 2nd-fret *B* for the V chord. For the fretted *A* try simulating the bar dips with half-step finger slides. You can also get the same effect without touching the bar: Bend the *A* string one and a half steps at, say, the 12th fret in place of the bar dips, while simultaneously picking the open-*E* riff. Try it and amaze your friends. (Note: This only works if your trem system is set up to "float" on two or three springs.)

Ex. 1a

Ex. 1b

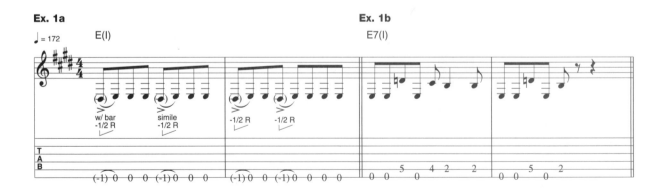

Ex. 1b is a typical two-bar surf riff; **Ex. 1c** transposes it to *A* to cover the IV chord. The full-barre *B* (V) and *A* (IV) chord punctuations in **Ex. 1d** recall "Wipe Out"—the rests between the chords were usually the drummer's spot to go fill-crazy. To form a 12-bar tune, play Ex. 1b twice, followed by Examples 1c, 1b, 1d, and 1a. You can preface this progression with an intro consisting of Ex. 1a played four times.

Ex. 1c

Ex. 1d

The tremolo-picked, palm-muted low-*E* glissando in **Ex. 2a** pops up in tune after tune, most notably preceding the signature *E*-minor figure in the Chanteys' "Pipeline" (**Ex. 2b**). This ultra-cool accompaniment, surf music's most recognizable riff, also appears on the group's follow-up, "Beyond," as well as in the Ventures' "Diamond Head" and the Avantis' "Gypsy Surfer." (Don't worry about hitting each note in the glissando exactly; the transcription simply illustrates the distance it covers.) The riff is transposed to *A* minor in bar 2 of Ex. 2b. **Ex. 3a** and **Ex. 3b**, both played with identical fingering, are complementary lead-guitar melodies.

Ex. 2a

Ex. 2b

Ex. 3a

Ex. 3b

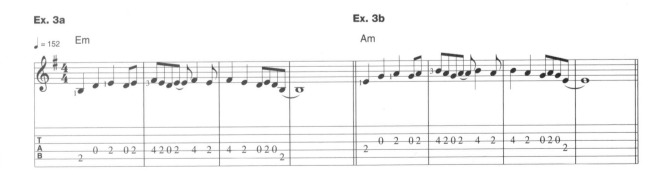

The use of 8- and 16-bar bridges helped surf tunes escape the standard 12-bar rut. The simple melody in **Ex. 4** outlines an *Am–G–F–E* progression (Im, ♭VII, ♭VI, V), primarily in chord tones.

Ex. 4

Shimmery sustained chords with watery trem-bar dips were another surf hallmark. **Ex. 5a** illustrates a ninth-position *A* triad voiced on the top three strings. **Ex. 5b** and **Ex. 5c** follow suit, switching inversions to form *D* (IV) and *E* (V) chords in the same vicinity. (The depth of the bend is transcribed on the first string; they vary on the other strings because of the differences in string size.) Piece together a 12-bar form by playing Ex. 5a twice, followed by Examples 5b, 5a, 5c, and 5a again. For contrast, try replacing the last four bars with **Ex. 5d**.

Ex. 5a   **Ex. 5b**   **Ex. 5c**

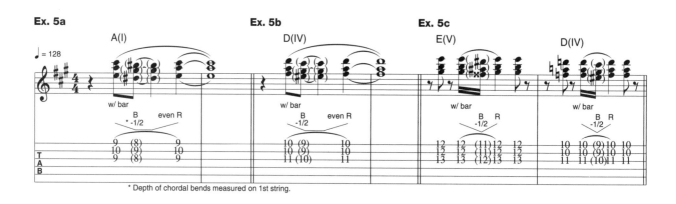

* Depth of chordal bends measured on 1st string.

Ex. 5d

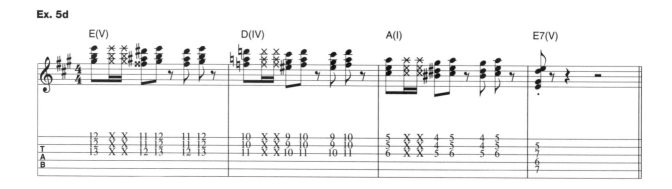

Ex. 6, also derived from chord tones, combines single-note and chordal bar dips in a typically cool melody with open strings aplenty. The bar dips applied to the ascending *Am* inversion are another surf staple. Tremolo-picked melodies (sometimes controlled, sometimes not) have graced many a surf tune. The manic minor-key excursion in **Ex. 7** predates the now cliché-heavy metal rhythm gallop by a quarter-century. And the out-of-control trem-picked double-stops in **Ex. 8** out-shred many of today's thrashers.

Ex. 6

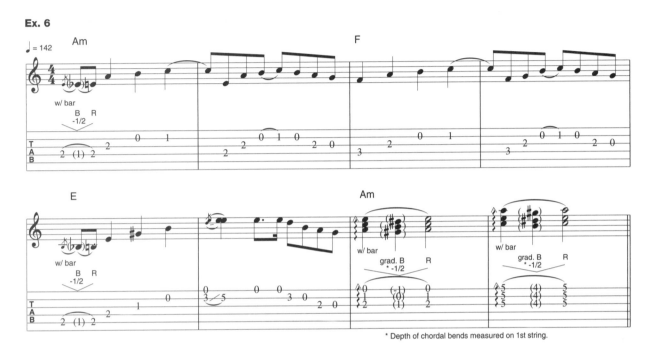

* Depth of chordal bends measured on 1st string.

Ex. 7

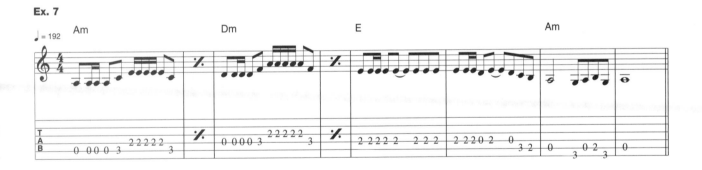

Ex. 8

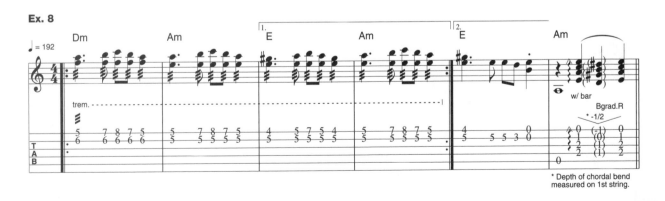

* Depth of chordal bend measured on 1st string.

Departing from the previous minor- and major-key I–IV–V progressions, **Ex. 9** grooves over an *E–D* (I–♭VII) Mixolydian-flavored vamp. Drown the notes in reverb. Release the muting for the twin response phrases beginning in bar 5. And dig the cool 10-bar form!

Ex. 9

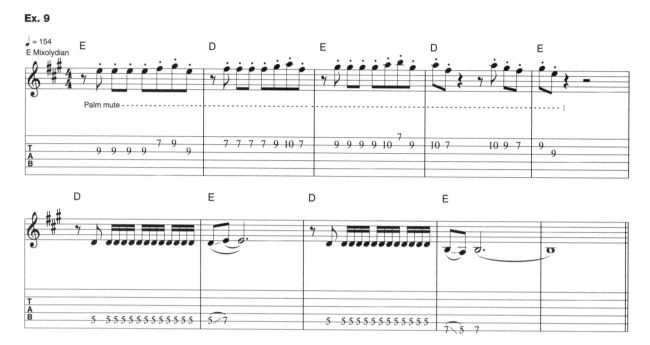

The rhythm figure in **Ex. 10** illustrates the quasi-Latin vibe evident in much surf music. Note the open-string, all-purpose passing chord on the last eighth-note of each measure. A Mediterranean influence is equally obvious in **Ex. 11**, based on the *A* harmonic minor scale (*A–B–C–D–E–F–G♯*) or, more specifically, its fifth mode, *E* Phrygian dominant (*E–F–G♯–A–B–C–D*).

Ex. 10

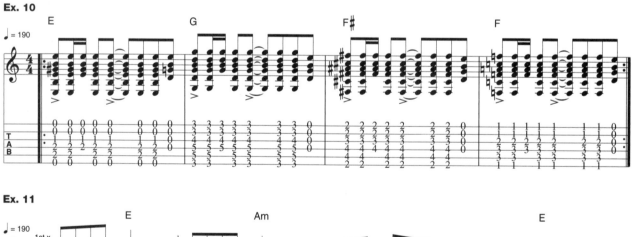

Ex. 11

Ex. 12 features a frenzied Dick Dale–style combination of trem picking, glissandi, and shifting time signatures (though you can count straight through in 4/4). **Ex. 13** coincides with my own passion for Martin Denny-style exotica. The arpeggiated *C♯m* and *Dm* create lush *E6* and *F6* harmonies over the Phrygian-derived *E–F* background harmony. And you can almost hear the fake bird calls as you play through the exotic melody in **Ex. 14**.

Surf's influence continued to show up in the music of composers as diverse as "Spaghetti Western" sonic architect Ennio Morricone, Frank Zappa, and Joe Satriani, and surf instrumental combos are riding a new wave of popularity. Not bad for a fad! ■

Ex. 12

Ex. 13

Ex. 14

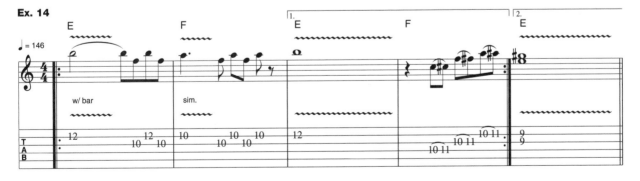

Joe Sia

Soaring with Skydog

DUANE ALLMAN

BY JESSE GRESS

A quarter-century after his passing, Duane Allman remains the unsurpassed king of rock slide guitar. Already steeped in the blues of Muddy Waters, Howlin' Wolf, Willie Dixon, B.B. King, Eric Clapton, and Jeff Beck, Duane became enamored with slide after hearing the late Jesse Ed Davis perform Blind Willie McTell's "Statesboro Blues" with Taj Mahal at an L.A. club. Using a glass bottle for a slide, Duane also began emulating Little Walter, Sonny Boy Williamson, and other blues harmonica players. In time, even his non-slide playing took on characteristics of his bottleneck style, as if both were becoming melded into one voice.

FREE Audio Version **Online**
www.PlayRock.TrueFire.com

Duane was obviously a fast learner with an uncanny grasp of open-*E* tuning, as heard on his records with the Allman Brothers Band and his soulful backing of Wilson Pickett, Aretha Franklin, King Curtis, John Hammond, Boz Scaggs, Clarence Carter, and others. Though he began playing bottleneck in standard tuning, Allman preferred open *E*, and he eventually limited his standard-tuned slide excursions to songs like "Dreams" and "Mountain Jam."

Early in 1970 the Brothers cut a studio version of "Statesboro Blues" in the key of *C*, while the later live *At the Fillmore* version was in *D*. A few months later, during the recording of *Idlewild South*, Allman tracked more cutting-edge, open-*E*-tuned electric slide on "Don't Keep Me Wonderin'" and "One More Ride." Continuing his studio work, he began to hit his stride later that year during Eric Clapton's *Layla* sessions. His bottleneck ranged from subdued to incendiary on eight of these tracks, almost all of which are in open *E* ("Layla" and "I Am Yours" are the exceptions). The *Layla* outtake "Mean Old World," a dobro duet with EC, is perhaps Duane's only recording in the more-rural open-*G* tuning. Duane's next big project, the Brothers' *At Fillmore East*, represents the pinnacle of bottleneck performance, The Book of electric slide.

Gear-wise, Duane favored Les Pauls, 50-watt Marshalls, and a glass Coricidin bottle worn over his ring finger. While sliding, he used his right-hand thumb, index, and middle fingers, which served double duty damping unwanted strings. Duane also used his left-hand 2nd and 1st fingers to damp behind the bottle. Low frets and medium-high action also helped. For accuracy like Duane's, align the tip of your ring finger directly over the fret.

Guitarists commonly use bends, hammer-ons, pull-offs, and finger slides to get from one note to the next. The slide imposes limitations on these techniques but offers several alternatives. In **Ex. 1a** both notes are fretted with the slide with no audible glissando in between. **Ex. 1b** features a picked grace-note slide into the second note, a motion performed with a single pick attack in **Ex. 1c**. Think blues harp for the even gliss in **Ex. 1d**. The grace-note slide preceding the first note of each previous example adds even more smoky harmonica flavor.

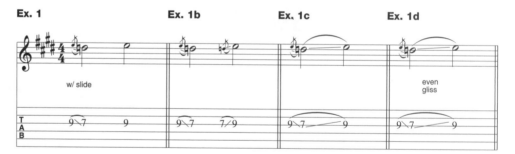

The advantages of open-*E* tuning are increased string tension (for more sustain) and economy of motion. Raising the open fifth and fourth strings a whole-step and the third string a half-step produces an open *E* chord (**Ex. 2a**), giving you, from low to high, the root, 5, root, 3, 5, and root. Since the root positions on the sixth and first strings remain unaffected, it's not necessary to relearn notes when moving the chord shape around the fingerboard. Using the slide to barre all six strings, this chord voicing may be transposed to 11 other fret

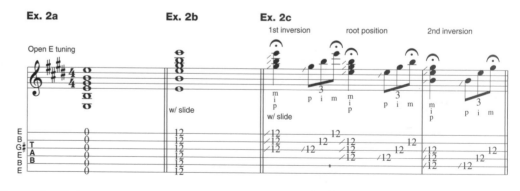

positions to accommodate chord changes or playing in different keys before recycling an octave higher (**Ex. 2b**). Open-*E* tuning also offers easy access to all three triad inversions, playable as chords or arpeggios. **Ex. 2c** demonstrates this while summarizing Duane's right-hand technique. For arpeggios, begin with the fingers resting on the strings as if you were about to play the entire chord, and then pluck each note individually.

When it came to spinning single-note lines (which made up 99 percent of his slide work), Duane preferred the urban "box" approach over more traditional open-string stylings. The box shape is formed by the addition of neighbor tones below the tonic chord position. **Ex. 3a** and **Ex. 3b** illustrate the lower neighbors (notated below the downward arrows) a whole-step below each chord tone. These lower neighbors (the lowered 7, 4, and 2/9) are incorporated into a typical Duane-style lick in **Ex. 3c**. **Ex. 4a** and **Ex. 4b** show the chromatic half-step neighbors (the natural 7, raised 4/lowered 5, and lowered 3), while **Ex. 4c** adapts them to the previous lick. In **Ex. 5** the same lick is treated to a combination of whole-step and chromatic lower neighbors.

Be sure to explore another important element of Duane's sound, the world of sweet 'n' sour microtones present between neighbor tones. Transpose these ideas over the entire fingerboard. Remember, Duane played fluently in any key.

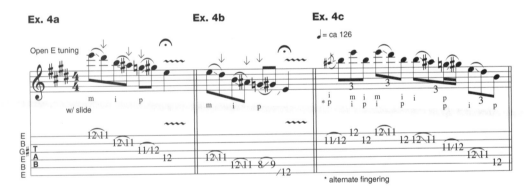

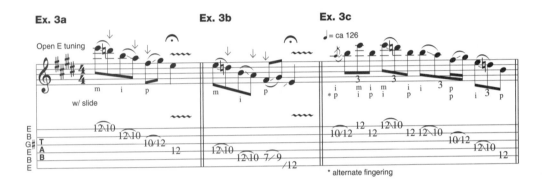

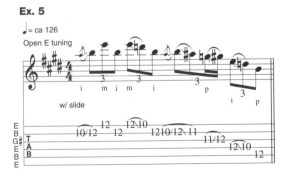

The next examples cover some of the building blocks of Duane's style. Each motif stands on its own and may be developed in many ways, including repetition, rhythmic displacement, elongation, and retrograde (reversing the order of the notes). **Ex. 6a** features a four-note motif moving across adjacent string groups with whole-step lower neighbors. **Ex. 6b** shows what a difference a subtle change in phrasing can make. **Examples 7a–7d** follow the same logic using a five-note motif. For some astonishing variations, replace the whole-step lower neighbors marked by asterisks with chromatic neighbors or in-between microtones.

Ex. 6a

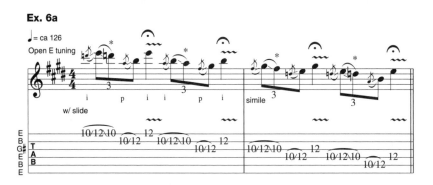

Ex. 6b

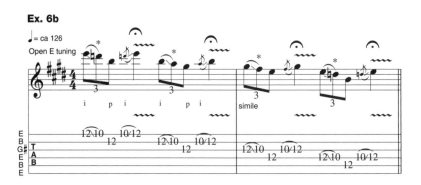

Ex. 7a   **Ex. 7b**

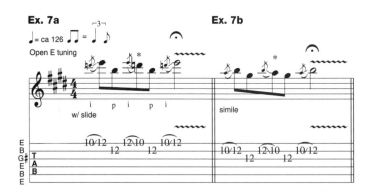

Ex. 7c   **Ex. 7d**

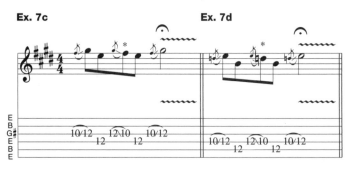

Neighbors *above* the tonic chord include the 2nd/9th, 6th, and 4th scale degrees. Duane used these sparingly, mostly as grace-note slides or for an occasional splash of pentatonic-major color. Instead, he'd extend the box by momentarily zipping up a major 3rd on the first or fourth strings, or by using the important minor-3rd spacing (only found between the second or third strings) to create a dominant 7 chord fragment three frets above the tonic. In the key of *E*, sliding up three frets from the tonic's *G* and *B* yields *B* and *D♯*, part of the *E7* chord (**Ex. 8a**). **Ex. 8b** shows the whole-step and chromatic neighbor possibilities for both two-note structures.

Ex. 8a   **Ex. 8b**

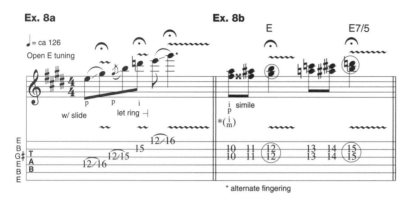

* alternate fingering

Culled from medium-tempo shuffles, Examples 9a–10b capture some of Duane's signature phrases. All have been transposed to *E* for you to mix and match. **Ex. 9a** is very harmonica-like. Add even more sass by exploiting those microtones. **Ex. 9b** uses the implied dominant 7 chord described above, and then outlines a descending box combining whole- and half-step lower neighbors. **Ex. 9c**'s chromatically ascending minor 3rds lead up to a signature major 3rd jump up the first string before the descending box/octave-leap conclusion. A similar move in **Ex. 10** navigates the IV–I change, as does **Ex. 10b**, a funky mid-register harp lick.

Ex. 9a

Ex. 9b

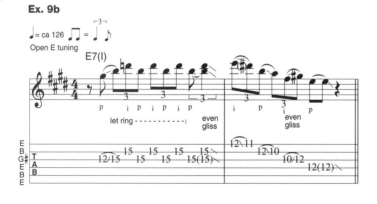

Ex. 9c

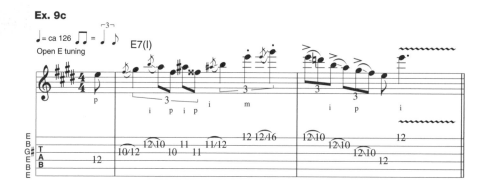

Ex. 10a

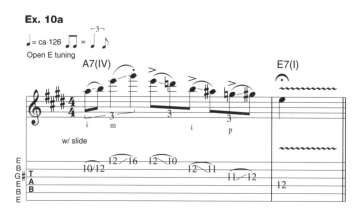

Ex. 10b

Transposed to the key of *D*, the blues harp outing in **Ex. 11** covers the last four measures of a 12-bar blues. Duane's flawless intonation is evident as he zips off the fingerboard to the hypothetical 26th fret. Move it up a whole step (to *E*) for a real trip into the stratosphere.

When bottlenecking in standard tuning, Duane often wove adventurous linear excursions up and down the string in place of the blues-box approach, perhaps partially influenced by his interest in jazz greats Miles Davis and John Coltrane. Duane's melodic development is masterful in **Ex. 12**, inspired by a videotaped performance of "Dreams." His two-bar call-and-response lines emphasize a 3/4 pulse, while the rhythm section lays down a 6/8 jazz waltz. ■

Ex. 11

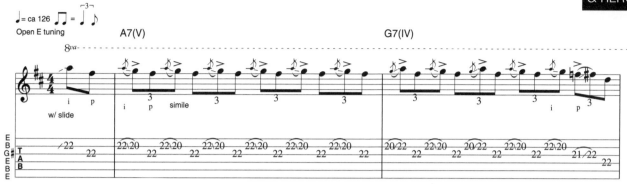

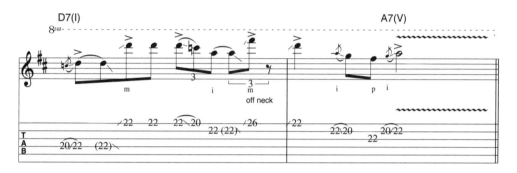

Ex. 12

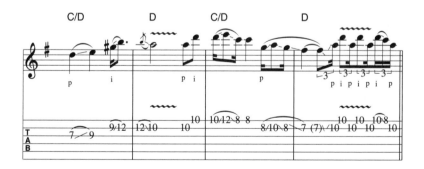

Angus Young of AC/DC

Lisa Sharken

Heavy Fretting

GET DOWN & DIRTY WITH MODERN RIFF MASTERS

BY ADAM LEVY

The spotlight doesn't usually fall on rhythm guitarists. It's the lead players who typically get the glory. And why not? The solos are where the drama and dynamics are—yet even the most astounding solos rarely incite toe tapping or head banging. No, for sheer physical impact, it's riffs that get the crowd rocking.

Think about it: Where would rock bands such as Black Sabbath or Led Zeppelin be without the indelible, river-deep riffs of "Iron Man" or "The Ocean"? And guitarheads might be more prone to rave about Eddie Van Halen's "Eruption," but again, it's his raucous riffs ("Unchained," "Hot for Teacher") that put the band on the radio and on MTV in the early and mid '80s.

So what makes a riff tick? Why do some have staying power, while others fade away into memoryland? Is there a fool-proof formula for winning riffs? The best way to answer these questions is to dissect the work of some of today's top riff merchants—newbies and hard-rocking veterans alike.

The Living End is a fairly young band, but the players must have skipped a grade at riff college because—in terms of relentless grooves and killer tones—these guys are way ahead of the class. Their 1999 album, *The Living End*, displayed their punkabilly roots—think Clash meets Reverend Horton Heat—with guitarist Chris Cheney playing his brains out with drop-dead rhythm work and hopped-up solos. On the band's 2001 release, *Roll On*, the rockabilly vibe is toned down, but the power-pop sensibilities have been focused to a laser-like intensity.

Ex. 1, based on the intro of "Riot on Broadway" (*Roll On*), recalls Bon Scott–era AC/DC, with widespread chords shifting over a tonic pedal-tone. (This example is reminiscent of AC/DC's "Riff Raff" intro.) After a bar and a half of similar motion, the chord-over-bass strategy gives way to a primal *A* minor pentatonic move, then settles on a standard-issue *A5* power chord.

Like our first Living End–style tidbit, **Ex. 2** (à la "Don't Shut the Gate," also from *Roll On*) is deceptively simple. It starts off with an *E5* power chord in the guitar's bottom range. The *E5* works up to *A5* (bar 1, beat *four*) via a blues-based bend and a pull-off, and eventually climbs up to *Bb5* (downbeat of bar 2). The riff's route back down to home base is less kinetic but just as effective. The rule here: Keep it simple.

Cheney's tone trip is straight-ahead: Gretsch guitars (usually a White Falcon or a Duo Jet) paired with Marshall or Soldano amps yielding a chimey grind similar to that of his Australian compatriots Angus and Malcolm Young of AC/DC.

Ex. 1

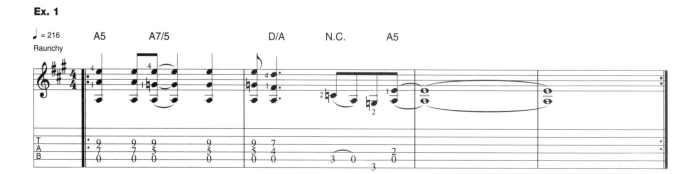

Ex. 2

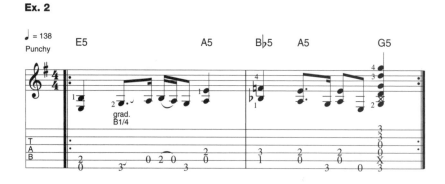

Speaking of AC/DC, the powerhouse Aussie quintet is no newcomer to the riff trade. Led by sibling guitarists Angus and Malcolm Young, AC/CD has been hard at work since the mid 1970s, tooling such radio-friendly rockers as "Highway to Hell" and "You Shook Me All Night Long." The band's 2000 release, *Stiff Upper Lip*, shows they haven't lost any of their infamous edge.

This little beauty (**Ex. 3**) was inspired by the intro from *Stiff Upper Lip*'s title cut. Like many of AC/DC's guitar hooks, this one has a playful vibe, but it means business. Let's take a look at the key elements. A tied-over eighth-note pickup anticipates bar 1's downbeat, and an eighth-note tie also jumps the bar's beat *three*. These anticipations provide drive. Another point of interest is the pedal-tone low *A* that rides below most of the riff. It, too, gets the horses under the hood galloping—and the wide gaps between the low *A*'s and the higher melody notes on the first and second strings add an expansive quality. The triads in bar 2 (*D* on the "and" of beat *one*, *C* on beat *three*) provide sweet contrast to bar 1's bluesier material.

To get yourself properly tuned into the AC/DC zone, play this example on a humbucker-loaded solidbody (Malcolm Young's fave is a '63 Gretsch Jet Firebird; Angus plays Gibson SGs), with a modicum of Marshall-style grind. Optional: Bob your head with reckless abandon.

Ex. 3

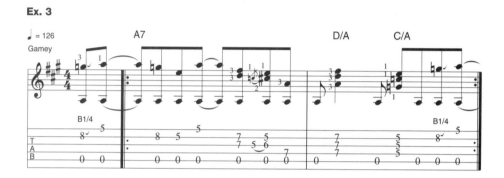

Opeth may not be a household name, but the band sure knows how to write 'em—wild power riffs with a few odd harmonic turns, that is. Peter Lindgren and Mikael Åkerfeldt make up the group's two-man guitar army, and on their album *Blackwater Park*, the pair alternate between arpeggiated acoustic niceties and full-metal-jacket assaults. Some of their most broiling riffage can be heard in "The Leper Affinity," on which **Ex. 4** is based.

These guys aren't afraid of harmonic tension. And they know that one of the easiest ways to sour a power chord is to add its ♭9, which is exactly what happens in bar 1, on the "and" of beat *one* and the ensuing five eighth-notes. (In this case, the chord is *E5*, and its ♭9 is *F♮*.) The tension gets resolved before the end of bar 1, as *E5* returns without the ♭9, but more acerbic harmonies ensue in bar 2. Beat *one* features a half-step slide into a tart *Gaug* triad (*G, B, D♯*), and the *Gaug* is followed by another augmented triad—*F♯aug* (*F♯, A♯, D*). The slide down from *D* (bar 2, beat *four*) releases the tension, but the four-note ascent (*E, G, B♭, D*) on beats *five* and *six* spells out an *Em7♭5* arpeggio, curdling the harmony once more.

Taking a broader look at the harmony of this example, you can see something particularly interesting. Scan the top note of each chord: Atop *E5*, we have *E*, on *E5♭9* is an *F*, and

Ex. 4

Riffin' It, Old School
Ten Classics You Need to Know

There are literally thousands of great songs to mine for riffs. If you're new to this territory—or if your long-term memory needs a little refresher—this short list can point you in the right direction for classic riffage.

1. **Johnny Burnette & the Rock 'n' Roll Trio**
   "Train Kept a Rollin'" (*Rockabilly Boogie*, Bear Family)
2. **Van Halen**
   "Ain't Talkin' 'Bout Love" (*Van Halen*, Warner Bros.)
3. **The Kinks**
   "All Day and All of the Night" (*The Story of the Kinks*, Donna)
4. **Aerosmith**
   "Walk This Way" (*Toys in the Attic*, Sony/Columbia)
5. **AC/DC**
   "Back in Black" (*Back in Black*, Atlantic)
6. **Led Zeppelin**
   "Heartbreaker" (*Led Zeppelin II*, Atlantic)
7. **Ozzy Osbourne**
   "Crazy Train" (*Blizzard of Oz*, Epic)
8. **The Beatles**
   "Day Tripper" (*1962–1966*, Capitol)
9. **Nirvana**
   "Smells Like Teen Spirit" (*Nevermind*, DGC)
10. **The Meters**
    "Cissy Strut" (*The Very Best of the Meters*, Rhino)

when *E5* returns, *E* is on top again. A *D♯* sits atop *Gaug*, and *D♮* (spelled enharmonically as *C* double-sharp) rides *F♯aug*. Strung together, that's *E, F, E, D♯, D*—a chromatic climb up and back from the tonic of our key (*E* minor) down to its ♭7 (*D*). This neat bit of voice-leading keeps our tweaky progression from being just a random, dissonant chord sequence.

This example is meant to be played with a touch of grinding distortion, but not too much. When you're dealing with tricky harmonies—anything other than power chords, really—using too much distortion can obscure your chords' intricacies.

Imagine early Black Sabbath tunes written from an entirely different lyrical mindset. The minor-pentatonic riffs are still in play and the guitar tones are still fuzzy and treble-free, but in place of Ozzy Osbourne's cabalistic poetry, the lyrics are filled with tales of cruising the streets in a tricked-out van. Getting the picture? Welcome to the world of Fu Manchu.

Fu Manchu guitarist/songwriter Scott Hill is a master of the bone-simple riff, as **Ex. 5**'s four-bar figure illustrates. Based on "Boogie Van" (from *King of the Road*), this spacious dropped-*D* item is built from notes of the *D* minor pentatonic scale—*D, F, G, A, C* (1, ♭3, 4, 5, ♭7). The inclusion of the *C♯* passing tone between *C* and *D* each time the line ascends and descends adds a bluesy chromaticism reminiscent of Led Zeppelin's "Black Dog" and "Custard Pie" riffs.

Check out how bars 2 and 4 differ slightly: Bar 2 ends on a low *G*; bar 4 ends on *G* an octave higher. This subtle change makes bars 3 and 4 sound like a "response" to the "call" of bars 1 and 2. Try starting this example on bar 3 for a cool variation. Played this way, the riff's response phrases go up first, then drop down low at the end (bar 2 is now bar 4).

For an appropriately Manchurian tone, run your favorite solidbody through the nearest fuzzbox (preferably a Big Muff) with the pedal's tone knob rolled way back.

Ex. 5

Nonpoint is a heavy-rocking foursome of young guns whose guitarist, Andrew Goldman, drives the band's songs with tight, chunky rhythms.

Let's dig into **Ex. 6**, a fierce figure similar to the one Goldman plays on "Mindtrip," on *Statement*. (Note: Goldman tunes *CGCFAD*, bottom to top—but we've written the example in dropped-*D*.) This syncopated riff bounces above the drum groove like a speedboat skipping across water. Check how in bar 1, the first two-beat phrase starts right on the downbeat, giving the phrase a strong, rooted feel. The second half of the bar (starting on beat three) begins with a 16th-note rest, giving an off-beat feel. We repeat bar 1's first half at the top of bar 2 (returning to more solid rhythmic ground), and then we're in for a surprise on beats *three* and *four*: The tight, 16th-based rhythms give way to a loping eighth-note-triplet descent. The effect of this groove-lurching maneuver is the rhythmic equivalent of downshifting—and you can feel how it jams the gears a little.

For Nonpoint-approved riffs, call up your favorite bone-crushing tone—then roll the gain back just a bit. While this example should sound heavy, too much dirt can cloud the progression. That's definitely something to consider when you're working down in the guitar's lowermost register and changing chords frequently.

Ex. 6

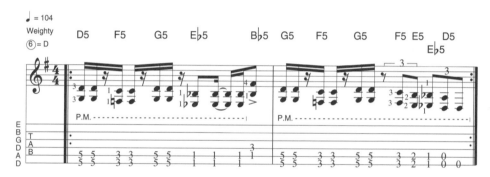

If a picture is truly worth a thousand words, the image of Ace Frehley tattooed on Dimebag Darrell's chest should tell you where Pantera's guitar man is coming from. Although his band's music and image are edgier than anything on Kiss's *Destroyer*, the idea is the same—if it rocks, it's good, and when in doubt, rock harder.

On Pantera's 2001 release, *Reinventing the Steel*, the group continues the tradition of chunk-style metal-rock it established on its breakthrough 1990 album, *Cowboys from Hell*. **Ex. 7**'s galloping figure is in the style of "Yesterday Don't Mean Sh**," from *Reinventing the Steel*. Sort of a demonic version of the James Bond theme, this twisted line sits entirely on the sixth string (tuned down to *D*). Like many of the riffs in this lesson, this line is somewhat repetitive, and that's part of its charm. The twist comes at the very end—in bar 2, on beat *four*.

Ex. 7

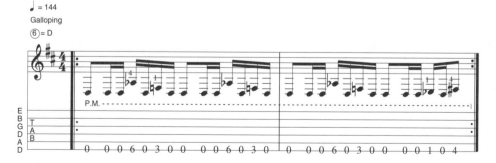

Here, the eighth-and-two-16ths rhythm used throughout the example is inverted, and two new notes are introduced—E♭ and F. If we put the notes of this riff in sequential order, we have D, E♭, F, F♯, and A♭. In the key of D, that's the root, ♭9, ♯9, 3, and ♭5. Except for the repeated root and the 3 (which only sounds once), it's all altered tones. Now *that's* the way to create harmonic tension.

This example's fret-hand fingering is also worth noting. You should use fingers 4 and 1 for most of this riff—at the 6th and 3rd frets, respectively. Then, on the beat *four* of bar 2, you reverse the fingering order (now 1 and 4) to nail the first and fourth frets. Though a listener may not appreciate the guitaristic "inside joke" at work here, your hand would wink at you if it could.

Our second Pantera-style riff, **Ex. 8**, is based on the main line from "Revolution Is My Name"—also from *Reinventing the Steel*. This little ditty nicely illustrates Darrell's unique blend of chunky speed-metal fervor and classic-rock vibe. It's played on the bottom three strings, all of which are tuned a whole-step below standard pitch (E down to D, A to G, D to C). You may want to tune all six of your guitar's strings down, but that's not necessary since you won't be using your treble strings.

Triplet rhythms are the backbone here. As with several of our other examples, the call-and-response element is crucial. Bar 1 is the basic "call," and bar 2's "response" is a cool sequence built from the D blues scale. (D, F, G, A♭, A, C.) Bar 3 calls again, with a quarter-note-triplet variation on bar 1's eighth-note-triplet figure. Bar 4's answer paraphrases bar 2, with bluesy, bent F♮ on beats *two* and *four*.

If you're looking to muster up a tone similar to Darrell's, go for a hard-edged, high-gain approach. (For the record, Darrell uses his Washburn signature models—based on the classic Dean ML design—and solid-state Randall amps.)

Ex. 8

I hope this lesson has opened your eyes, ears, and fingers to some new riffing possibilities. If you want to take it further, try writing your own variations on each riff. Ask yourself, "If this is the song's opener, what would sound good in the next section?" Another approach is to keep one of the example's rhythmic elements intact while changing most or all of the pitches. (For instance, Ex. 5's D blues line could be reworked into a G Lydian or E♭ minor line.) Of course, you can always start from scratch—just pick up your guitar, crank into your favorite tuning, dial up a righteous tone, and go for it. Rock on. ∎

Brian May of Queen

Joe Sia

Twin Tones & Layered Lines

HOW TO CREATE & ARRANGE HARMONIZED GUITAR PARTS

BY ANDY ELLIS

Whether it's sweet and singing or rude and searing, the sound of guitars locked in harmony is powerful and seductive. Fortunately, it's not difficult to create this dimensional effect. Once you understand a few basic techniques, you'll be able to arrange harmonized guitar parts and insert them into your own music. To that end, let's analyze a handful of classic twin-guitar passages inspired by the Allman Brothers Band, Steely Dan, Thin Lizzy, the Eagles, Fleetwood Mac, Humble Pie, and the maestro of track layering, Brian May.

FREE
Audio Version
Online
www.PlayRock.TrueFire.com

Armed with one guitar and a beady set of eyes, you can suss out the following examples. But to really get down with harmonized guitar, you'll want to haul out a multi-track recorder or invite a guitar-totin' friend along for the ride. Hearing both parts together, you'll make a crucial discovery: It's not just the intervals, but the enriched texture that's responsible for creating twin-guitar magic.

Thin Lizzy's "The Boys Are Back in Town" features tough yet melodic harmony played by Brian Robertson and Scott Gorham. Inspired by the 16-bar twin-guitar solo, the sparse and horn-like **Ex. 1** begins with 3rds: C#–E (minor 3rd) and A–C# (major 3rd). While major and minor 3rds form the backbone of many harmonized lines, other intervals add intriguing colors. For example, bar 3 begins with a tritone (G–C#). Comprising three whole-steps, this edgy interval outlines an A7 by stating its ♭7 (G) and 3 (C#). In bar 3, the line drifts into parallel 4ths (A–D and B–E) before settling down to a minor 3rd (F#–A) in bar 4.

Take some time to get acquainted with these intervals—the major and minor 3rds, the perfect 4ths, and the tritone. The more quickly you can recognize them sonically and visually, the easier it will be to master guitar harmony.

Some performance tips: The top line (Gtr. 1) sounds cool played with a round, sustaining tone. Pick the bottom line (Gtr. 2) closer to the bridge to keep it crisp and distinct. It's a fast rock shuffle, so feel the underlying eighth-note pulse like this: *dah*-do, *dah*-do.

Ex. 1

The Allman Brothers Band's Duane Allman and Dickey Betts epitomize twin-guitar harmony, and **Ex. 2**—inspired by "Revival (Love Is Everywhere)"—illustrates the elegant contours of their timeless duets. The phrase is primarily composed of perfect 4ths. Unlike 3rds, which imply either a major or minor tonality, 4ths sound ambiguous, restless, and a bit exotic. At three points, however, this ambiguity gets grounded by major 3rds: C–E (on the "and" of beat *two*, in bars 1 and 3), and the vibrato-laden A–C# (at the end of the four-bar phrase).

Except for the final C#, each line is built exclusively from the A minor pentatonic scale, yet—thanks to the 4ths—the sound isn't bluesy. Despite the song's brisk tempo, Allman and Betts manage to sound loose and relaxed.

Play each part with a clean, flutey tone.

Ex. 2

♩ = 176-184
Brisk & relaxed

The original Fleetwood Mac featured cool twin-guitar interplay by Peter Green and Danny Kirwin. Inspired by "Coming Your Way," **Ex. 3** offers a flash of their sonic magic. This eight-bar riff comprises a pair of repeated two-bar phrases. These "cells" begin in unison—two eighth-notes in the first phrase; three eighth-notes in the second. It's a cool trick: Each phrase seems to bloom as it progresses.

Bar 2 consists entirely of 5ths (*E–B, D–A,* and *B–F♯*), and another 5th appears in bar 4 (*F♯–C♯*). Like 4ths, 5ths don't give the music major or minor flavors. The difference is that 5ths sound open and stable, while 4ths sound clangy and beg for resolution.

Other riff highlights include a pungent major 2nd (*A–B*) in bar 1, a 4th (*F♯–B*) in bar 1, bluesy minor 7ths (*E–D*) in bars 3 and 4, a major 6th (*D–B*) in bar 4, and octave *B*'s in bar 4. No shortage of color here!

To nail the distinctive Mac sound, add quick, quivering vibrato to those bends.

Ex. 3

♩ = 138-144
Sweet & singing

Steve Hunter and Dick Wagner kick off the live version of Lou Reed's "Sweet Jane" with a soaring duet based on the four-bar phrase in **Ex. 4**. The riff consists mostly of minor and major 3rds (*E–G* and *D–F*, and *C–E* and *Bb–D*, respectively), but an occasional 4th (*G–C*) adds spice to the thick, ringing sound.

Check out bar 2's quarter-note triplets. This three-against-four rhythm sounds especially epic when played in blazing harmony. Also notice how Gtr. 1 has grace-note hammers (bars 2 and 4) that aren't mirrored in Gtr. 2. Such small differences add flair to a harmonized phrase without detracting from its unified sound.

Ex. 4

In "Hotel California," the Eagles' Joe Walsh and Don Felder use another cool technique to create a three-against-four feel. The basic idea is a no-brainer: Simply arpeggiate a series of triads starting on different chord tones, and the harmony will automatically emerge in 3rds and 4ths. The tricky bit lies in the tumbling rhythm, which rolls a three-note arpeggio across beats that have been evenly subdivided into 16th- or eighth-notes.

The secret is revealed in **Ex. 5**. Look at the shifting accents: Because they occur on every fourth note, they effectively carve the long string of tones into three-note packets. Notice

Ex. 5

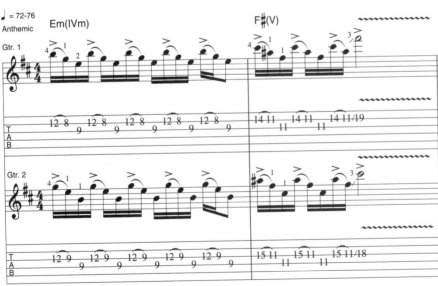

how we squeeze five *Em* arpeggios into bar 1, followed by three *F♯* arpeggios in bar 2. (In the third *F♯* arpeggio, the final note jumps up an octave.)

The kinetic logic that drives these parts becomes apparent when you play them, and you'll find the moves intuitive and finger-friendly. Thanks to the incessant pull-offs in this example, your 4th finger will get a serious workout, so take it easy.

Pentatonic scales and arpeggiated triads provide useful tools for generating harmonized guitar parts, but sometimes a snazzy chord progression demands a more linear strategy. Take **Ex. 6**, for instance, which is inspired by the turnaround in the Allman Brothers' "Hot 'Lanta."

In bars 1 and 2, four minor-7th chords descend chromatically. Allman and Betts simply track the progression in minor 3rds: Gtr. 1 targets the ♭3 in each chord while Gtr. 2 plays the respective roots. This yields two stepwise lines—*G, F♯, F♮, E,* and *E, D♯, D♮,* and *C♯*—that underpin the passage. Notice how the savvy bros carefully insert a few additional notes to break up the straight descent and add melodic interest. Likewise, the hammer (bar 1) and bend (bar 2) supply rhythmic variation.

Ex. 6

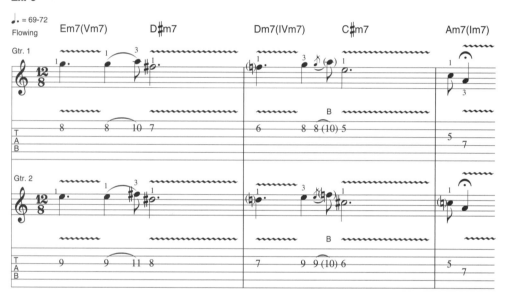

Tips for Tracking Twin-Tone Lines

When you're layering harmonized lines in the studio, try to synchronize your attacks. Your harmony will carry maximum punch if the notes hit simultaneously. But having uniform timing doesn't mean your rhythms have to be square: Groove the first part any way you want—just make sure the subsequent overdubs lock up to it.

You'll get a full, lush sound if each line has a unique tone. These differences can be subtle: Each time you track a new part, switch pickup settings, or pick closer to the fretboard or bridge, or simply swap picks. For more dramatic timbral contrasts, change your guitar, amp, or effects, or try playing one line with a slide.

It's a good idea to record the primary melody first—it sets the sonic stage—and then fill in the supporting parts one layer at a time. If you have more than two tracks of guitar, it's wise to gradually reduce ornamentation—the hammers, pulls, slides, and bends—as you build your harmony. Another tip: Reserve the ear candy for the thinner strings, and let the thicker strings provide the beef. And for maximum protein, try doubling each part.

During mixdown, you can enhance the distinction between two lines by separating them in the stereo panorama. Lines that are rhythmically tight sound especially cool panned wide. Conversely, to make loose parts sound more cohesive, pan them closer.

There's no law that says dual guitar lines have to share the same melodic contours or rhythms. In Humble Pie's live "Four Day Creep," for instance, Steve Marriott and Peter Frampton often head in entirely different directions. **Ex. 7** offers a glimpse of this action: While Marriott (Gtr. 2) plays a straight blues riff—think Jimmy Reed meets Jimmy Page—Frampton rips into an extended *E* Mixolydian (*E*, *F♯*, *G♯*, *A*, *B*, *C♯*, *D*, or 1, 2, 3, 4, 5, 6, ♭7) phrase. The music is raw and spontaneous, yet the parts fit like a glove.

Notice the contrary motion in bar 2's first beats. Frampton climbs in eighth-note triplets and Marriott descends in quarter-notes. Ultimately, Marriott hits a low *E*, while three octaves above, Frampton outlines an *E* chord by playing *B* (the 5) and then *G♯* (the 3).

Ex. 7

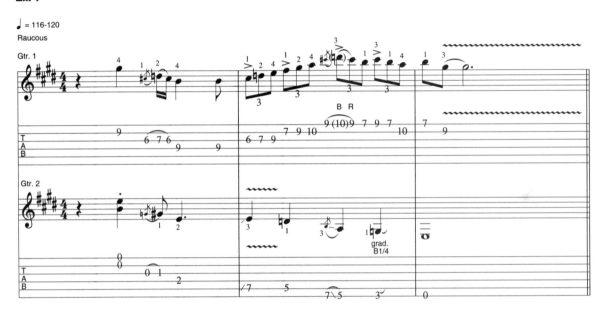

Ex. 8

On the same Humble Pie album (the essential *Performance—Rockin' the Fillmore*), Frampton and Marriott use another cool trick in Dr. John's "I Walk on Gilded Splinters." **Ex. 8** captures the moves: Each guitarist plays a line composed of sixth interval shapes. Because these lines begin a minor 3rd apart, we hear four-note harmony.

While shifting positions within each line, keep both fingers glued to the strings as much as possible. This will help you hear and see the major- and minor-6th shapes as you pluck them.

Though less common than twin-guitar parts, triple-tracked lines sound amazing. Steely Dan's "Bodhisattva" features such rubbery harmony, courtesy of Denny Dias and Jeff Baxter. **Ex. 9** offers a four-bar snapshot of this electric choir.

Scope it out—the intervals are all major and minor 3rds. If you analyze the harmony, you'll find a chord on each beat: *G7* (*B–D–F*), *C* (*C–E–G*), *Dm* (*D–F–A*), *Am* (*A–C–E*), *G* (*G–B–D*), and *F* (*F–A–C*). But you couldn't get this singing, bowed effect by simply strumming these three-note voicings. Nope, the parts must be tracked as independent lines with their own bends, releases, pulls, hammers, and slides.

Ex. 9

♩ = 200–208

Fat & sassy

[musical notation: Gtr. 1, Gtr. 2, Gtr. 3 with standard notation and tablature]

Who knows more about layering harmonized guitar lines than Brian May? Derived from Queen's "Bicycle Race," **Ex. 10** illustrates his cunning creativity. In this example, the two guitars play an elaborate game of hide-and-seek.

In bar 1, Gtr. 1 climbs through a *D* major scale. On the last eighth-note, Gtr. 2 chimes in with an *A* Mixolydian (*A, B, C♯, D, E, F♯, G*) run that rises through bar 2. May repeats this exchange and then picks up the pace in the next two bars by alternating snippets of *D* and

B major scales on every two beats. Bar 7 gets even more intense as the guitars swap half-step hammers before arcing into a tart major-2nd bend (*E–F#*).

Take your time working out this eight-bar passage. To make it sound righteous, you'll need to play with pinpoint accuracy.

Ex. 10

Once you've digested these examples, you're ready to develop your own harmony parts—either with other guitarists or by multi-tracking à la Brian May. As you experiment, keep these tips in mind:

• To create a rich chordal tapestry, use a mix of major and minor 3rds laced with occasional 4ths. Or, for a more open sound, try layering major and minor 6ths (which are inverted 3rds).

• When you want to be harmonically ambiguous, use 4ths and 5ths. 4ths are restless, 5ths are stable.

• For extra sparkle, work in an occasional major 2nd, minor 7th, or major 9th.

• Octaves and unisons add muscle without suggesting a counterline.

• Great twin-guitar harmony results from layering intriguing melodies, so think horizontally. Your textures will be vibrant and inspiring if each part sounds cool by itself. ■

Ken Settle

Deep Pockets

TOM MORELLO TESTIFIES ON SIMPLE RIFFS & HEAVY GROOVES

BY MATT BLACKETT

FREE Audio Version Online

www.PlayRock.TrueFire.com

Once a guitar freak, always a guitar freak. Rage Against the Machine's Tom Morello can't change who he is—someone who likes nothing better than to sit around and jam. And, although you're not likely to hear him do it on a Rage album, this guy burns. After demonstrating an example for this lesson, he often let fly furious scale runs that would sound at home on a fusion record. Morello's stocks in trade, however, are heavy-funk riffs and strange sounds, and those are what he delivers here. I played some beats on a boom box, and asked Morello to improvise riffs—just as he would when jamming with his band.

"This chord riff might not be applicable to a Rage tune," says Morello about **Ex. 1**. "To make it work for us, I'd probably put some space into it and try to make it more mechanical sounding." Playing over a funky beat, Morello dips liberally from the Hendrix well to find his pentatonic fills and double-stop stabs. Notice how he turns the riff around differently each time he plays it, which accounts for the four endings. Lay back—being too anxious will make this example sound stiff.

Ex. 1

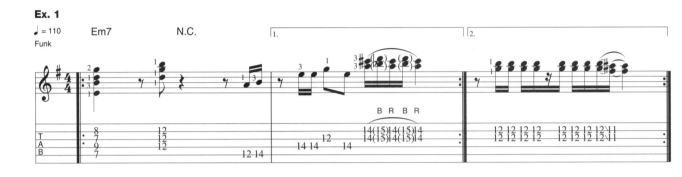

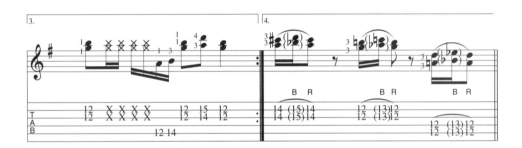

A big part of Morello's style revolves around sonic experiments, and chief among them is his use of toggle-switch gating. To do this, you'll need a guitar with at least two pickups, and—most important—separate volume knobs for the two pickups (stock Strat cats need not apply). The basic premise is to have your bridge pickup volume on 10 and your neck pickup completely off. Hit a note or a chord, wiggle the toggle switch back and forth, and listen

Noise Notes

The song "Voice of the Voiceless" from *The Battle of Los Angeles* features an intriguing flute-like tone and a very non-Rage major tonality. We already know Morello can take notes played on the guitar and morph them into noises with no semblance of—or need for—melody. On this tune, however, he takes a noise and plays an entire melody without ever fretting a note.

The line's seemingly infinite sustain suggests an EBow, but that move would be too obvious for Morello: "To create the sustain I laid in front of my amp and got my guitar feeding back on the open G string. With the feedback wailing, I played the melody using my right hand to rotate the pitch preset knob on my Whammy pedal. You can still hear the open G droning as I go through the preset pitches, so it kind of sounds like a bagpipe line. Those big jumps are just me accidentally hitting the two-octave setting on the knob. To pull this off live, I had Ibanez build the guts of a Whammy pedal into a guitar."

to the stuttering burst of sound. **Ex. 2a** shows the difference between what you're doing with the toggle (notated above the staff), what you hear (top staff), and what your fretting hand is actually doing (bottom staff and tab). Your fretting hand is simply holding an *E* whole-note, while the picking hand works 32nd-notes on the toggle switch. Because every upstroke of the toggle produces silence, you end up with 16th-notes. Cool, huh?

Ex. 2a

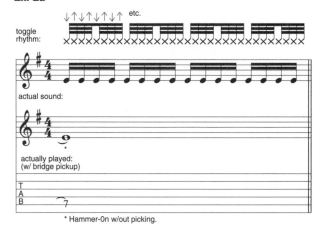

* Hammer-0n w/out picking.

Things get hairier in **Ex. 2b**. To recreate Morello's relatively simple line, you'll need to hammer or pull every new note because your picking hand will be working the toggle switch. This is one of those techniques that's harder to notate and describe than it is to play, so just give it a try. Let your ears guide your hands.

Ex. 2b

Once again for **Ex. 3**, the line you hear (marked "actual sound") is just a simple, three-note repeating figure. Keep that rhythm in your head as you toggle through the lick. This technique is so cool that once you start, it almost doesn't matter what you play.

Ex. 3

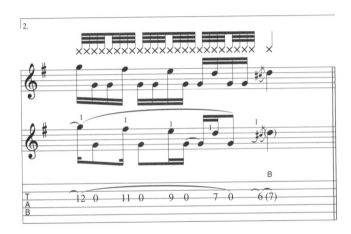

When I punch in an eighth-note rock beat, Morello grabs his Strat and busts out the dropped-*D* funk of **Ex. 4**. He plays every part of this riff just a touch behind the beat, so relax and let the music breathe—just be sure to really slam the one-finger power chords in bar 3. Bar 4's downbeat is an open string, so you can hang onto the *C5* that precedes it until the last possible second.

Ex. 4

Ex. 5 is another dropped-*D* riff, and it's full of funky scratches. To nail this, you'll only need your 1st and 3rd fretting fingers playing at the 3rd and 5th frets. "When it comes to riffage," says Morello, "I'm all about these two fingers and these two frets. Finding variation and power in a few simple notes has always been key for us." It's simple, but that doesn't mean it's easy. The lone 16th-note in the first ending can take you by surprise if you're not careful. But if your drummer catches that accent with you, look out!

Ex. 5

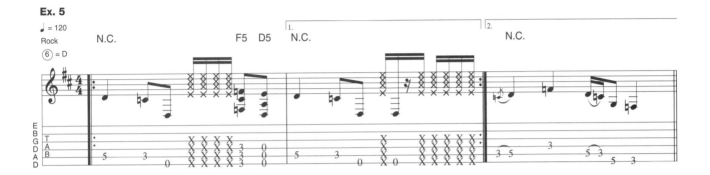

Ex. 6 and **Ex. 7** are breakdown sections for the tune Morello started in Ex. 5. To create the scratchy syncopations, Morello keeps his right hand moving in a constant 16th-note rhythm, and he accents the groove by just missing the strings occasionally. To add a bit of otherworldliness, he strums behind the nut on beat *four* of bar 2 in Ex. 6. "When I'm coming up with a second part, I tend to err on the side of deconstruction. I also like to leave gaps for the vocal. That makes it heavier when the rock comes back in." ■

Ex. 6

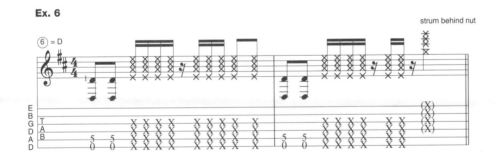

Ex. 7

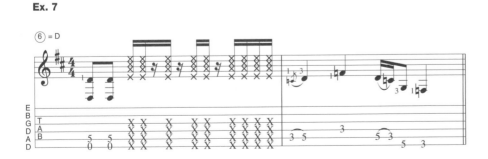

Meegs Rascon
of Coal Chamber

Nikki George

Subterranean Soul

DIG THE RUMBLE & CLANG
OF DETUNED GUITAR

BY ANDY ELLIS

Though low-tuned guitars were introduced back in the '50s, the sound of slack strings rumbles louder than ever in today's music. From grinding rock to twangy country, pickers of all persuasions are digging the rich, wiry sound of a detuned ax. Some folks get down on a 7-string (tuned *B, E, A, D, G, B, E*), while others draw heaviosity from a baritone—a 6-string guitar tuned down a 5th to *A* (*A, D, G, C, E, A*) or down a 4th to *B* (*B, E, A, D, F♯, B*). Still other players develop their own unconventional "deep 6" tunings, like Coal Chamber's Meegs Rascon, who tunes his B.C. Rich to B, E, A, D, G, B (like the bottom six strings of a 7-string), or System of a Down's Daron Malakian, who parks his Ibanez Iceman at C, G, C, F, A, D (that's dropped-D tuning, lowered a whole-step).

This lesson celebrates the many flavors of subterranean soul with a collection of riffs that we've reworked for B baritone. We settled on this format (as opposed to, say, 7-string or A baritone) for two reasons:

• Availability. You don't need a new guitar to explore the twangy world of baritone. If you have an underutilized standard 6-string, you can transform it into a baritone with little effort or expense (see DIY Baritone Conversion, below). A standard guitar, with its relatively short string scale, sounds better as a B bari than an A bari.

• Adaptability. The bottom four strings of a B baritone are tuned identically to a 7-string's bottom four strings—B, E, A, D. Because the riffs in this lesson fall on the baritone's lowest strings, you can also play all these examples on a 7-string. Read the tab as written (simply pretend strings 6, 5, 4, 3 are strings 7, 6, 5, 4) and voilà—instant 7-string conversion.

DIY Baritone Conversion

It's not hard to convert a standard electric guitar into a deep-twangin' baritone. First, a few caveats: True baritones have a longer string scale than your average guitar—typically between 27" and 29". Therefore, Stratocasters and Telecasters—with their 25 ½" scale—are better candidates for conversion than, say, a Les Paul, with its relatively short 24¾" scale. Bari conversions generally won't sound as twangy as their long-scale siblings, and the lowest string on a short-scale conversion won't intonate perfectly beyond the 9th fret or so. (This is not a issue as long you stick to the lower positions when fretting the sixth string.) That said, some guitarists prefer playing short-scale conversions because the fret spacing feels more natural than that of an elongated neck.

Wrenching

To transform a regular guitar into a baritone, begin by simply restringing with the gauges suggested below. (Through trial and error, you'll be able to customize the gauges to suit your playing style.) The lower four strings are wound; only the top two are plain.

You'll need to widen the nut slots and then do a setup—tightening the trussrod, adjusting saddle height, and intonating the strings—see Guitar Repair, page 89. (Another reason Fender-style guitars make better conversions is because you can easily replace their nuts if you want to return your guitar to its standard-tuning setup.) You'll also want to lower your pickups to compensate for the increased string mass. Back them down a quarter of a screw-turn, then listen to a few open chords. When they have a rich, full clang and a lingering sustain, you're there.

On some instruments, the new sixth string may be too stout to thread into its tuner post. If so, remove the tuner and have a machine shop enlarge the hole a tad. I've successfully converted a Fender Standard American Strat to a B baritone, and even a .065 bottom string slips into its stock tuner with no hassle.

Other Options

With its extended scale length, a true baritone sounds awesome. And they're not that expensive: Danelectro's basic model lists for under $400. Companies such as Jerry Jones and ESP offer cool baritones for less than $1,000. Alternatively, you can retrofit a long-scale neck onto most guitars with bolt-on necks. Warmoth (www.warmoth.com) and WD Music Products (www.wdmusicproducts.com) make baritone necks designed to couple with Strat or Tele bodies for $150 to $250.

B Baritone String Chart

string	6	5	4	3	2	1
pitch	B	E	A	D	F#	B
gauge	.058W	.048W	.038W	.028W	.018P	.014P

Our riffs are inspired by a variety of bands and players, ranging from such 7-stringers as Munky and Head of Korn to the baritone-wielding, honky-tonkin' Pete Anderson. For this lesson, let's put aside any stylistic prejudices and simply celebrate the art of low.

For starters, we have to deal with a bit of transposition. **Ex. 1a** shows how the standard guitar's open strings are notated—*E, A, D, G, B, E*, from low to high. To notate the *B* baritone's open strings—whose deep tones ring a 4th lower—we have to sink into the bass clef or wallow in ledger lines, as in **Ex. 1b**.

But there's a better way: Let's simply write the bari's notes another octave higher, so they fall handily on the treble clef, as in **Ex. 1c**. Wow—no ledger-line or bass-clef insanity. The tab keeps us oriented on the fretboard, and the "*8vb*" marking between the notation and tab staves reminds us that the music actually sounds an octave lower. Perfect! (Theory fans will want to read So Where the Heck *Are* We?, page 79, to sort out the real difference between what we're reading and hearing.)

Ex. 1a

Standard tuning

Ex. 1b

B baritone tuning

Ex. 1c

B baritone tuning written one octave higher

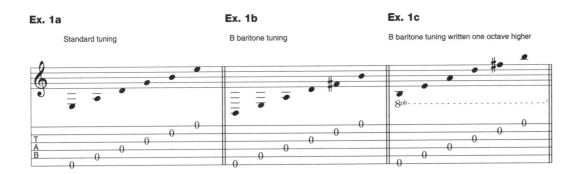

Inspired by the grinding riff in Coal Chamber's "Sway," **Ex. 2** is easy and fun to play. It introduces two key moves: First is beat *two*'s "hammered power chord." In this elastic interval, the top note remains constant, while the bottom note alternates between the fretted root and the open string. We'll encounter variations of this maneuver throughout the lesson. The second move is the upward half-step shift that occurs on the "and" of beat *four*. Many heavy riffs rely on this momentary twitch to create tension and release. To make Ex. 2 sound menacing, lean into those accents and use plenty of dark, broiling distortion.

Ex. 2

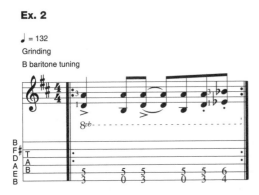

Part of the rockabilly classic "Train Kept a Rollin'," **Ex. 3** illustrates the timelessness of rock guitar. More than 50 years ago this riff introduced the hammered power chord to the first generation of rockers, and it connects Coal Chamber to Johnny Burnette & the Rock 'n' Roll Trio, by way of the Yardbirds and Aerosmith.

What's new, however, is the subterranean setting—"Train Kept a Rollin'" sounds massive when pitched this low. After repeating the two-bar phrase as written, slide the power chord up two frets from *D* (third position) to *E* (fifth position). Don't change your rhythm, and keep hammering the open *B* string. After a bar of *E*, return to *D* for a measure. (You can complete the riff by sliding through *E*, *F#*, *E*, *D*, and *C#* power chords rooted on the 5th, 7th, 5th, 3rd, and 2nd frets, respectively.)

Ex. 3

For another twist on the hammered power chord, try **Ex. 4**—a nod to the brooding riffs in Korn's "Beg for Me." Though we've dropped down a fret to work out of a second-position *C#* power chord, the hammered moves are similar to those in the previous two *D*-based riffs. As before, we hold the top note and move between an open string and fretted root below it.

The new bits come at the end of each bar, where we punctuate the chunky power chords with chimey open fourth (*A*) and third (*D*) strings. Check this out: If we slid the *C#* power chord up a half-step (borrowing Ex. 2's tension-and-release move), we'd be darting in and out of a *D* power chord (*D–A*). Ex. 4's open *A* and *D* strings are simply an inversion of the "half-step-up" power chord. Because you can let them sustain momentarily against *C#*, you get even more tension and release.

This riff's groove is denser than the previous two, but its tempo is considerably slower, so the strumming action won't overwhelm you. Use a palm mute to tamp down the bottom strings. See the staccato marks on those last two intervals in bar 4? Though they incorporate open strings, you can control their duration. Using a quick wrist snap, pick the notes, and then cut them off abruptly with the karate edge of your picking hand.

Ex. 4

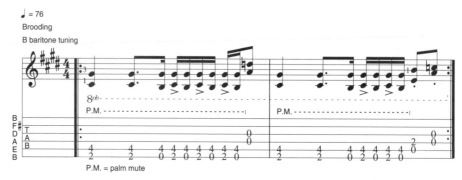

Derived from a riff in Limp Bizkit's "My Generation," **Ex. 5** also revolves around the second position. This figure requires a clean tone. Palm mute all notes except for the final *D* (bar 2, beat *four*), which you should play with heavy finger vibrato. Snap the first two beats in each bar like a '70s funk bass player.

It's fun to play this hypnotic riff into a looping device—such as a Boomerang or Line 6's DL4 pedal— and then improvise over the recycling phrase. You'll find *C#* Aeolian (*C#*, *D#*, *E*, *F#*, *G#*, *A*, *B*, *C#*) works nicely.

Ex. 5

So Where the Heck *Are* We?

Traditionally, the guitar is notated an octave higher than it sounds. With the exception of a few mavericks—such as jazzbo Johnny Smith—guitarists have done this for the past two centuries. Why? If we were to write guitar music in its true register, we'd probably be reading both bass *and* treble clefs, like pianists. We think of middle C as being on the 3rd fret, fifth string—because that's how we notate it—but sonically, middle C is on the 1st fret, second string. Confused? Hang on, it gets better.

The *B* baritone is tuned a 4th below standard guitar. To avoid all the ledger lines that would result from writing baritone riffs a 4th below the guitar, we've bumped our bari notation up an octave so it sits neatly on the treble clef. But remember, because guitar is already notated an octave higher than it sounds, this means that we're actually notating the baritone *two* octaves above its true pitch.

It's no big deal, really. How we notate our instrument doesn't change how we play it. In fact, many pickers don't even realize that there's any transposition involved with regular guitar. But now *you* know.

To see how baritone relates to guitar and bass (as well as other family members), refer to the tuning chart below. From low to high, the open strings for each tuning are shown horizontally and identified by pitch and string number.

Tuning Comparison Chart

6-string guitar			E (6)	A (5)	D (4)	G (3)	B (2)	E (1)
7-string guitar		B (7)	E (6)	A (5)	D (4)	G (3)	B (2)	E (1)
B baritone guitar		B (6)	E (5)	A (4)	D (3)	F# (2)	B (1)	
B baritone, dropped-A		A (6)	E (5)	A (4)	D (3)	F# (2)	B (1)	
A baritone guitar		A (6)	D (5)	G (4)	C (3)	E (2)	A (1)	
6-string "tic-tac" bass	E (6)	A (5)	D (4)	G (3)	B (2)	E (1)		
4-string bass	E (4)	A (3)	D (2)	G (1)				

The pensive, clangy riff from System of a Down's "Spiders" adapts beautifully to *B* baritone, as shown in **Ex. 6**. Go easy on the low-*B* pedal tone—don't let it drown out the fourth string's melody. Pick carefully and strive for a clear, legato sound. Pay attention to the accents—they bring dimension to this eight-bar passage.

Ex. 6

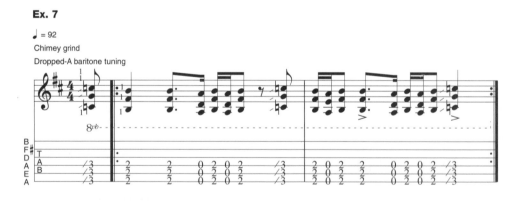

You can add girth to a standard guitar by lowering its sixth string a whole-step from *E* to *D*. This dropped-*D* tuning (*D*, *A*, *D*, *G*, *B*, *E*) drives many mighty riffs, but when it comes to moving air, you can't beat dropped-*A* tuning on a *B* baritone guitar. The principle is the same—simply lower the sixth string a whole-step—but the resulting *A*, *E*, *A*, *D*, *F♯*, *B* sounds like dropped-*D* on steroids.

Korn's "Trash" inspired the moves in **Ex. 7**. Thanks to the dropped-*A* tuning, you can fret all the power chords with your 1st finger. Notice the half-step slide at the end of each measure—it's similar to the upward shift we first tried in Ex. 2, but this time we're gripping three strings. Sonically, shoot for thick, distorted lows capped with a hint of sparkling highs. It helps to scoop out the midrange.

Ex. 7

Ex. 7 draws power from its stuttering rhythm, as does **Ex. 8**, another dropped-*A* crusher. Derived from Korn's "Counting," Ex. 8 makes a cool one-bar loop. To make this lurching riff fly, however, you need to contrast its legato slides with its sudden rests, and your timing has to be precise. The secret is to play the rests—approach them like you would a note or chord. Many guitarists seem impatient with silence and rush through it, but you can't create gut-wrenching riffage if you're in a hurry.

Ex. 8

Virtually any dropped-*D* riff sounds super played on a dropped-*A* baritone. For instance, let's recast Neil Young's cosmic "Cinnamon Girl" riff (**Ex. 9**). Because it covers a large fretboard area, "Cinnamon Girl" is dandy for auditioning baritone guitars at your local music store. It sounds great played loud with a gritty tone. See if you can insert some 7th-fret harmonics in bars 1 and 3.

In Dwight Yoakam's hard-swinging "Little Ways," Pete Anderson gets down on an ultratwangy low-strung guitar. To recreate his lines in dropped-*A* bari tuning, play **Ex. 10**. Coax bar 3's quarter-bends from your slackened sixth string—don't rush them.

Ex. 9

Ex. 10

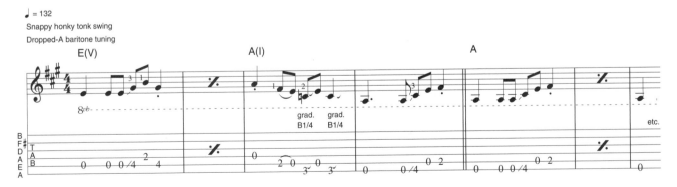

If you play baritone, sooner or later someone will ask if you know the theme from Twin Peaks. Angelo Badalamenti composed the line, but we can thank the session-guitar innovator Vinnie Bell for its vibey twang. **Ex. 11** shows how to finger the theme in *B* baritone tuning. The phrase is easy to play, but it's a challenge to cop its tone. Use reverb and a fast, strong tremolo, and for extra snap, pick near the bridge.

Ex. 11

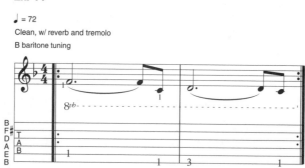

And while we're on the subject of TV themes, who can resist picking the Peter Gunn riff on low, twangy strings? Roy Buchanan, Jimi Hendrix, Dick Dale, and the Hellecasters all recorded some variation of Henry Mancini's catchy theme, but for **Ex. 12**, we'll pay homage to Duane Eddy by including his two-bar call-and-response intro.

We're in the key of *B*. In Mancini's original recording, the riff ends on a ♭3 (in this key, *D#*). Oh—way too square. Like Dick Dale, let's replace both 3s with ♭3s (*D♮*), and goose them with quarter-bends. Dale also caresses the 2 (here, *C#*) with a quarter-bend to suggest the ♭3, so we'll do that, too.

Ex. 12

To explore the differences between guitar and baritone, we've focused on the bari's low notes. You can, however, create lovely sounds by playing a baritone up in the guitar register. Standard guitar voicings and lines sound impossibly rich duplicated on a baritone, due to its thicker strings and longer scale. (Of course, the latter only applies if you're playing a real baritone, as opposed to a converted guitar.)

Here's a final thought: Armed with a capo and a baritone, you can create fat, cello-like rhythm parts in the studio—without dipping below the guitar's range. Played this way, baritone can be a stealth tone machine. ■

30 Ways to Sound Better

BIG-TIME TONE SECRETS FOR STAGE & STUDIO

BY THE *GUITAR PLAYER* STAFF

Tone is guitarists' Holy Grail. And though Sir Galahad undertook his quest in solitude, you don't have to venture off alone. After all, there are myriad tone mavens who have already made the quest, slain the dragon, grabbed the chalice, and discovered the secrets of great sound. All you have to do is follow in their footsteps. To help you with your search for transcendent tone, we've assembled a "Round Table" of sonic knights— from famous guitarists and renowned repairmen to manufacturers and engineers—and asked them to share their tips, treatments, and methods. Happy hunting.

VISUALIZE
ELLIOT EASTON
When you're attempting to come up with parts and cool sounds, envision the sound you want before you try to create it. I never pick up a guitar until I know exactly what I want to do.

USE YOUR ROOMS
PETER LEWIS
When recording at home, use every live surface you've got—bathrooms, the kitchen—as chambers. Rooms can add more character than you'll get from a digital effects processor.

USE THE ROOM
GEORGE MARTIN, PRODUCER

I'm a great believer in getting the sound right in the studio. If that works, the rest is easy. A room is an instrument, and it affects the other instruments. If you understand what your guitar sound is like "in the raw," you'll have a much better idea of how it should be "cooked."

ROLL YOUR OWN
REEVES GABRELS, DAVID BOWIE COLLABORATOR

Cut a 50-cent-piece-sized hole in the bottom of a coffee can and put a Shure SM57 with a foam collar around it inside the can. Place the can against the speaker or some distance away— you'll get a unique resonance. You can also use toilet paper and paper towel rolls; just jam the mic into the end of the roll. It's like a comb-filter EQ, but not as heavy-handed; it's more like cupping a hand to your ear. It's the same effect you get with phase cancellation and mic placement.

Jerry Garcia on Tone

" My concept of good tone is a clear, unambiguous sound on each note. For me, that means relatively high frets, heavy strings, and a thick pick, so that your touch is coming from the hand and not from the pick. That's as basic as it gets." —*Guitar Player*, July '88

FEED YOUR HEAD
STEVE VAI

Sounding better is mostly in your head. The next time you sit down to play, sit in silence for a few moments and try to imagine how you want to sound. I'm not referring so much to amp settings or anything technical—I'm referring to the way your fingers hit the strings. Keep that audible image in your mind when you're playing, and focus to achieve it. It's also very important to record yourself and listen back with a critical ear. That way you'll be able to mold yourself around your own tastes rather than someone else's.

BE LESS THAN PERFECT
TCHAD BLAKE, PRODUCER

Technicians in the music industry dictate a certain perfection of time and tone. But things don't necessarily have to be that even, tight, or in tune. Now we have perfectly even computer-designed sounds, but they aren't as interesting as instruments with quirks. I like guitars with twisted necks. I like buzzes and fret noise. I like when one note sounds great, but the next one frets out like a sitar. The human mind is geared toward hearing anomalies. That's what keeps things interesting. Those sounds command attention.

OPTIMIZE YOUR GUITAR
TERRY MCINTURFF, TERRY C. MCINTURFF GUITARS

Experienced audio engineers know it's essential to have a good sound source to obtain great tones. Guitarists can ensure the best tone for any situation if their sound source—the guitar— is performing to its maximum potential. Locate an experienced luthier who can help you keep your guitar in great shape. Seek recommendations from fellow guitarists, and pay a visit to the luthier's shop to get a feel for the craftsperson. A luthier who understands your musical requirements and whose shop has a professional vibe and reputation is a good bet. Remember—you are seeking the ideal doctor for your precious guitar. Check references and trust your instincts.

STRIP DOWN
DAVE CELL BLOCK, CELL BLOCK 5

The Old School punk tone is raw and stripped down—there's no candy-coated stuff—so stay away from pedals and gadgets. Get a Marshall head, crank it to 10, and plug in a Les Paul. I record with two Marshall half-stacks. One is in a small isolation booth for a compressed sound, and the other is set up in a hallway for natural reverb. The hall sound is brighter and cuts through the mix, while the room sound produces a fat bottom.

GO DIRECT
LINDSEY BUCKINGHAM

On *Out of the Cradle* I was dealing with a certain amount of layering. Direct recording allowed me to contain individual sounds as much as possible and give each sound its own character. It allowed me to get a dense sound when everything was layered together, but still retain clarity.

EMULATE
JOE GORE, SESSION GUITARIST, *GUITAR PLAYER* CONSULTING EDITOR

With a good speaker emulator, you can instantly replicate the sound of a well-miked cabinet. The tones are vastly more amp-like than any direct-to-the-board preamps I've tried. After all, you're using the preamp and power-amp sections of your favorite amp. You can get tape-frying tones at sensible volumes.

USE A MIC OR TWO
JUSTIN BROADRICK, GODFLESH

I sometimes record demos with the guitars direct, but never the records—it's always a little too fizzy direct. I drive my Marshall hard and use two mics, usually Shure SM57s: one really close, and another farther away. I use an idea I read in a classical music magazine years ago: I walk around the room, use my ear to pick a favorite spot, and stick a mic there. That way, I get the ambience with the room mic and the extreme top end from the mic close to the speaker cone. I'll mix those two mikes together for one take, and then double the track with exactly the same setup. Then I pan those two tracks out hard left and right to create the biggest wall I possibly can.

DON'T READ ABOUT IT!
DAVE NAVARRO

Reading a magazine article never helped me play or sound better—playing helped me sound better. An hour or two of practicing in my room has always been more effective and productive than learning what kind of amp Carlos Santana uses.

FOLLOW THE SONG
MIKE TURNER, OUR LADY PEACE

The first concern of any guitarist should always be the song. The song will dictate the part, and the part will dictate the tone—so pay attention! After that, the most important things are to play in time, play in tune, and play musically. People tend to overlook these three simple things in the search for the ultimate tone. At some point in a tonal obsession, you become more of an engineer than a guitar player. You're there to play guitar, so just use your ears and do it.

MESS UP YOUR PICKS

DAN ERLEWINE, *THE GUITAR PLAYER REPAIR GUIDE; HOW TO MAKE YOUR ELECTRIC GUITAR PLAY GREAT!*

Some of my favorite tones are produced with worn flatpicks. When a flatpick's edge gets rough, it produces a wonderfully aggressive biting effect similar to a bow being drawn across violin strings. When I really want to make my strings sing, I reach for an old pick. You can reproduce this effect by sanding the pick edges with 220-grit sandpaper, but nothing beats natural pick wear. I'll also use a common hole punch to create a hole in the center of the pick. This keeps the pick from slipping, turning, or losing position as I'm playing—and I love the feel of my index finger touching the flesh of my thumb.

GO CHEAP

REEVES GABRELS

Put a cheap, low-rated 12" speaker in a good enclosure and record it in a closet. That way, you can get the speaker to distress easily. You can also get great results with tiny practice amps or even Radio Shack intercoms—all you need is a mini-jack adapter for your guitar cable.

TAKE THE SHORT ROUTE

PETER LEWIS, ENGINEER/PRODUCER (ROD STEWART, VAN DYKE PARKS, BRIAN SETZER)

People use too many miles of cable in the studio—that adds noise. The cleanest and simplest signal path is the most important factor. Also, you need to learn your listening environment. This will help you determine how your finished results will sound when you're listening to material in your car, through headphones, on somebody else's stereo, or in an A&R office. A good engineer needs to know what the final mix is going to sound like everywhere.

SWAP PREAMP TUBES

MARK BAIER, VICTORIA AMPLIFIER CO.

While most guitarists are aware of the influence that power tubes have on amplifier performance, many overlook the importance of preamp tubes. Proper preamp tube selection is critical to bringing out the best in your amp. Take time to acquaint yourself with the sonic nuances of different brands of tubes in the same tube family. For instance, there are dozens of different brands and vintages of 12AX7s available. By learning their sonic characteristics, you will be able to better calibrate your amplifier for your specific needs.

Often, swapping the modern Russian or Chinese 12AX7s found in most new amps with quality NOS (new old stock) varieties can turn a bland-sounding amp into something much more musical and intuitive-sounding. Start by swapping tubes in one socket only—preferably the first input tube—and listen carefully to a familiar lick or chord progression. You'll be surprised at the contribution this one tube can make. And don't overlook the tubes in your rack gear or tube-driven footpedals. The next time you get a jones to spend $300 for a pair of RCA Blackplates or Mullard EL34s, remember the same money can buy a dozen or more quality NOS "peanut" tubes.

KILL THE REVERB

BRENT MASON, SESSION PRO

One thing live players have a tough time doing when they get into the studio is turning off the reverb. (I had to go to Reverbaholics Anonymous!) Reverb can mask your sound so it doesn't cut through the track enough to really pop—and once you track with reverb, it can't be removed. Your parts will jump out a lot better if you cut them dry.

FLIP THE PICK
CRAIG CHAQUICO

Use the round edge instead of the pointy part of your pick to get a fatter tone for solos. This is the opposite of getting high, harmonic squeals from the pick and finger, and the technique works best with heavy-gauge picks and strings. (I prefer the sound of Jim Dunlop Polycarbonate Gel picks and Dean Markley medium-gauge Blue Steel Cryogenic strings.) You can experiment with finding different sweet spots on the pick, and for a little more attack, you can score little grooves in the rounded part of the pick with a file or razor blade. I've used this pick trick on both electric and acoustic solos, but the technique can really be heard on the solo in "Jane" [Jefferson Starship's *Freedom at Point Zero*].

GO VINTAGE
SUSAN TEDESCHI

Use vintage amps to ensure a warm, fat tone, and plug directly into the amplifier—no crazy boxes! Play with your fingers and a pick. You can bring the sound down for a quiet solo by using your fingers, and then get loud and crazy with the pick. And always play like yourself. People who try to copy other players just end up sounding stupid.

PENCIL IT IN
GARY BRAWER, GUITAR TECH AND LUTHIER

The two main causes of tuning problems are not putting on new strings correctly (and not stretching them) and an improperly slotted nut. The first fix is obvious—get a lesson on string winding and make sure you stretch them out. The second fix is to have the nut slots checked and possibly filed out to the correct diameter and angled for each string. But one thing you can do yourself that eliminates a ton of tuning problems is to simply lift the string out of the nut and turn a pencil in the slot. The thin layer of graphite dust acts as a lubricant to keep the string from binding.

Eddie Van Halen on Gear

❝ Too many guys think that a certain player's sound has to do with equipment. But it doesn't really matter what you're playing through—your sound is in your fingers and brain."
—*Guitar Player*, July '84

CRANK IT UP
BILLY SIEGEL, FENDER MUSICAL INSTRUMENTS

Tone is a very subjective issue, but if I have any recommendation for guitarists, it's to turn up—especially when using tube amplification! These days some guitar players seem afraid to turn up their amps, but there's a tremendous amount of tonal responsiveness that comes from a cranked amp. A loud amp lets you use your guitar's volume and tone controls to go from clean to mildly distorted to totally in your face, and everywhere in between.

VENTILATE!
SAL TRENTINO, SAL TRENTINO ELECTRONICS

Give your amp plenty of ventilation. An easy way of accomplishing the cooling process is to purchase a small table fan at a discount store and place the fan behind the amp, blowing into it. The cooler your amp runs, the longer it will run. Your capacitors will especially love you if you keep them cool. And never place your amp with its back against a wall—this severely limits natural ventilation.

ADJUST YOUR SINGLE-COILS
HARVEY CITRON, CITRON GUITARS AND BASSES

When adjusting pickup height on a Strat, the greatest presence occurs when the pickup is as close as possible to the strings. However, the magnetic pull of Fender pickups is so great that it can inhibit vibration—causing poor intonation and sustain—if the pickups are too close to the strings. It's a balancing act. With this in mind, set the bridge pickup as close to the strings as you like, making sure to adjust the tilt for even response. Next, set the height of the middle pickup to match the volume output of the bridge pickup—checking the balance of all the string levels again—and repeat the process with the neck pickup. Adjusting the pickups this way will give you the best in-between tones as well.

TRY A PAPER CLIP
MIKE VIOLA, MIKE VIOLA AND THE CANDY BUTCHERS

If you want a little extra bite in your tone, put down your guitar pick and use a paper clip. I gave up my picks years ago in favor of a .038-gauge paper clip.

USE SPACE
YOGI, BUCKCHERRY

If you're looking for a shortcut to sounding better, you won't find it in the latest gadget. Of course it's important to use quality equipment, but don't waste too much time relying on gear. Your audience will be listening to the statement your guitar makes via your convictions and musicality. Don't assault your listeners with too much musical information—such as 1,000 meaningless notes. Make use of the economy of notes and utilize space, and you'll affect your listeners with greater impact.

MATCH YOUR AMP AND GUITAR
WILL RAY, HELLECASTERS

Not all guitars will sound good with your favorite amps—you have to find the right matches. Line up all your amps in a semi-circle, then plug straight into your first amp—no effects. Tweak the controls until you get a good sound. Now, turn the amp's master volume control up and down and note where the amp sounds best. Finally, plug into your favorite pedals and really listen to see if your pedals enhance the amp sound or make you suck big time. I see a lot of kids trading in perfectly good guitars and amps because they can't get a good sound, when in fact their pedals are to blame. After listening to the first amp with all your different guitars and effects—taking note of which combinations sound best—go to the next amp and do the same tests. When you're all done, auction off the losers and get some better stuff.

STUDY YOUR SIGNAL CHAIN
PAUL REED SMITH, PRS

If you're really serious about getting good tone, you have to audition every single piece in your signal chain. Each thing in that chain—from your hands to the guitar, strings, cord, stompboxes, amp, and speakers, and if you're recording, the microphone, mic position, mic preamp, and so on—makes a difference in the sound and is an art form unto itself. You can simply plug in a different cable and it literally sounds as if you're playing a different guitar. Players who are famous for their tone—Eric Clapton, Eric Johnson, and most of the guys who have been on the cover of *Guitar Player*—are extremely particular about this chain. They don't grab any old thing and say, "I just get a sound." ■

Guitar Repair

WHEN TO DO IT YOURSELF

BY DAN ERLEWINE

Guitarists tend to regard an instrument as something sacred. You've spent a lot of money for it, and it does seem sort of complicated if you don't know much about it. While guitar techs are always happy to get your business, there are plenty of little "repairs"—maintenance tasks, actually—that you can do yourself. You shouldn't be afraid of your instrument; serious players typically spend hours tweaking the action on their guitars.

One of the best ways to avoid repair bills is to spend more time buying the guitar in the first place. Instead of spending $2,500 for six different guitars before you finally get your first good one, learn more about the instrument and buy the best guitar you can afford to start with.

When you go to buy an acoustic guitar, for example, take along a mirror so you can look inside and see how well the guitar is built. If you are dealing with a quality instrument, you can expect to find good workmanship, but people who buy cheaper guitars sometimes have problems with them because they didn't check out what they were buying.

Learn how guitars are built so you'll recognize such things as warped necks, loose frets, and loose braces. Even some brand-name guitars are made with unseasoned wood, causing problems that make them play poorly. Before you go shopping you should also buy a guitar repair book, such as Hideo Kamimoto's *Guitar Repair* (Music Sales), and of course my own *Guitar Player Repair Guide* and *How to Make Your Electric Guitar Play Great!* (Backbeat). [For information on choosing a guitar, check Backbeat's *How to Play Guitar.*]

ADJUSTING A TRUSSROD

Anyone who can operate a microwave oven or a CD player should be able to adjust a neck rod by using a little common sense and reading up on the task at hand. Simple tools like allen wrenches, nut drivers, and screwdrivers are all that's needed, but study the books to find out what sizes you need—and to learn which way to turn the adjusting nut. As a rule, if you tighten the nut, the neck will straighten out. If you go the other way, it will loosen up and go with the pull of the strings (introducing "relief" into the fretboard). You shouldn't be afraid to do this.

Some necks play their best when adjusted perfectly straight; others need a small amount of "relief" to give the string extra clearance over the fret tops—especially toward the center of the string's vibration arc—to keep from buzzing. So if you sight down the neck from the nut toward the body and see a little dip around the 9th or 10th fret, it's probably relief. My personal choice is a rather straight neck on any guitar unless there are buzzes that I can't play around or remove by fret leveling. When all else fails, I'll adjust a little relief into the neck as a last resort—again, this is a personal choice.

REPLACING TUNERS

This is something you shouldn't do yourself, unless you're installing exact retrofit tuners. In the shop we see too many cracked pegheads where people have tried to drill out the hole with a hand drill. The best way to do it is to use a clamp and drill press or a hand reamer and round file.

Don't oil your tuning pegs. Oil seeps through the screw holes that hold the tuner and into the back of the peghead, causing the wood to swell and even split or crack. Most modern tuners are permanently lubricated and sealed and shouldn't be oiled anyway. If you have open-gear tuners that are stiff, smear a tiny bit of petroleum jelly onto the gears.

CLEANING THE FRETBOARD

I don't use any spray or stick lubricants on the fretboard, and never have—I find them much too slippery. I prefer simply to keep the fretboard and strings clean. Clean the fretboard periodically with a dry rag. If the frets are well seated, there's no reason you can't use a damp (not wet!) rag and soap to loosen grime—soap and water can clean anything on a guitar if you're careful, especially on an electric. If there's too much built-up dirt, use some extra-fine (0000) steel wool pressed into the edge of the fret with your thumbnail. Occasionally, perhaps once or twice a year, work a small amount of lemon oil into the fretboard. Don't put anything on maple fretboards, because they're lacquered. Use only cloth to clean them—steel wool will scratch.

As for removing all the strings to clean the fretboard, it does upset the tension balance on an acoustic guitar, but it's not a big deal with electric guitars. When I'm removing strings on a delicate vintage acoustic guitar, I prefer to introduce the loss of tension gradually by detuning slowly. I tune down to D and play it for a while, and then tune down to C and play it, and finally remove the strings.

When you change strings, adjust a trussrod, or do anything to a good-playing guitar (especially acoustics), expect to wait a few days for the instrument to settle back into peak playing form. A smart tech gets a guitar done days before the customer comes to pick it up, so it will sound at least as good as it did when they brought it in—hopefully better.

NUTS

Nut and bridge setup has a great effect on your guitar's sound and playability. It's hard to make a good nut, and it takes some time, so don't expect your repair shop to just pull one out of a drawer and send you off down the street.

Each string should come up gradually over the nut and have its contact point right at the front of the nut. With most factory nuts and nuts from a drawer at a music store, you can't even tell where the string is making contact because it's down too deep in the groove.

The string slots should angle slightly toward the pegs, so that the string will go where it naturally wants to lie. I like to relieve the sides of my nut grooves away from the string, so they are not pinching and muting it. You need a lot of different size files to make nuts (Stewart-MacDonald has a good starter set).

A really nice nut won't last forever. If you hone it down carefully—so it's comfortable to play in the first position but doesn't buzz—it will wear out in time, regardless of the material it's made of. You'll have to shim it up or have another nut made. If your nut makes a "chinking" sound when you tune, and you're unable to smooth and shape a slot that's pinching a string, lubricate it with a little petroleum jelly or Teflon-lube.

BRIDGE SETUP

You'll be happiest if you learn to adjust your own intonation, because it's something you you'll need to do often. (For instance, each change in string gauge usually requires a read-justment of the bridge saddles.) After all, it's your own ear you're tuning to, right? My ear is different from yours. I can make a guitar play really in tune, and when I go out and play a job, it sounds great to me. But that doesn't mean that you'll like it.

Make this adjustment on each string: If the string sounds sharp when you compare the fretted note at the 12th fret with the open harmonic at the 12th fret, move the individual saddle back, away from the neck; if the string sounds flat, adjust the saddle forward.

It's easy to clean the bridge parts on most electric guitars. Take the bridge apart and clean the pieces with naphtha or lighter fluid. (Wear rubber gloves when working with these kinds of solvents.) Get all the grease off the parts, put them back together, and then lightly lubri-cate any working surfaces with thin oil (sewing machine oil is nice), and your bridge will work well again.

As for substituting one type of bridge for another, you should avoid pulling bridge studs and moving bridge parts around, like trying to put a Tune-O-Matic on a guitar that doesn't have one. And be very careful when putting a stop tailpiece on a Gibson ES-335 that has a trapeze tailpiece—you might install it crooked. Take that job to a pro.

Most bridge inserts, or "saddles," have pretty rough castings—they're not machined per-fectly, and the string slots are filed quickly at the factory. Many people have to replace the bridge pieces on their brand-new guitars because the string spacings aren't right, or the strings are too close to the edge of the fretboard, or they don't go over the polepieces properly, or they break easily. Most Fender-style bridge saddles don't require string slots because they're cast into the saddle. Tune-O-Matic–style bridges usually require a slot to be cut into the insert.

Simply changing bridge saddles isn't very hard. Buy a new set of saddles, take your bridge apart, put the pieces on, and reset the intonation. If your guitar plays in good tune before you remove the saddles, make a note of each saddle location so you can return to it with the new saddles. If you're replacing Gibson-style saddles, which need slots cut, buy a little set of needle files to cut the slots, and some 400- or 600-grade sandpaper to smooth the slots when you're done filing.

Although most tremolo adjustments are fairly easy, they're beyond the scope of this arti-cle. In brief, keep any friction points clean and lubricated with a light grease. To keep a tremo-lo guitar with a traditional (non-locking) nut in tune, you must have a properly made nut that doesn't pinch the strings.

As for acoustic bridges, I don't recommend do-it-yourselfers attempt bridge repairs on a flat-top guitar. If you can remove the saddle and would like to reshape it, that's fine (it's sort of like slotting your own electric bridge saddles), but don't attempt to remove or reglue a bridge—take that job to a pro.

Keep an eye on the back edge of an acoustic bridge; if it's coming loose you'll see a gap between the bridge and the top. Take a string envelope and try to slide the flap under any part of the bridge. If you can slip it under there, get it checked out. At our shop we see lots of bridges that could have been fixed more easily (sometimes better) when they first started coming loose.

DON'T FRET

Refretting and dressing frets is the most important job a guitar tech can do. Like bridge reglu-ing, this is something you shouldn't try yourself. And before you have your frets dressed or redone, spend some time trying different string gauges to find out what you really like. Then be sure the tech knows what kind of strings you use—that's critical. If you get a refret and setup and then drastically change string gauges, it's not going to play the same without a fresh setup.

I fret guitars using a jig that puts tension on the neck and holds it at concert pitch when the strings are removed. The body is also held so there is no spring-back. When I take strings off a Les Paul, for example, the neck will bow up a bit because of the trussrod tension. When I loosen the rod, it sets right back down on the tension jig's neck supports. That is right about where the neck will be when you play it. Then I take the frets out and get rid of any humps or bumps by judiciously leveling the fretboard.

When gauged with a straightedge, the upper register of the fretboard (from the 10th to the last fret) should be flat, or even fall slightly away from the straightedge. Many guitars "hump" a bit in that area, which causes string buzz. So there's more to a refret job than just pulling out the frets and hammering in new ones. Put your money into a good fret job and you'll never be sorry.

PICKUP ADJUSTMENT

Adjusting pickup height is definitely a job you can and should do—you've got to please yourself. Raise and lower the pickup height until you like what you hear. You'll know when you get the pickups too high—the strings will hit them. Fender-style pickups generally don't have individually adjustable polepieces; Gibson-style humbuckers and P-90 types have polepieces that can be raised or lowered individually to accommodate different gauges and wound or unwound strings. If you have a vintage guitar with adjustable polepieces that are rusted, don't try to turn them—take it to the shop.

Adjust the height of Gibson-style pickups with both volume knobs wide open. Switch back and forth between pickups while adjusting the height until the volume of both is equal. Then *back off* the neck pickup a little bit—being at the end of the string, the bridge pickup tends to be a little weaker than the neck pickup. The Gibson factory usually sets the pickups with a clearance of 3/32" on the neck pickup and 1/16" on the bridge pickup (clearance is measured between the bottom of the string, fretted at the last fret, and the top of the polepiece).

With Stratocasters, if you're willing to lower the pickups as far away from the strings as possible, they'll sound their best and you'll get more accurate noting. The magnets are so powerful that when you fret in the upper areas (especially on the low E and A strings), the magnets pull the strings out of tune.

There are a great number pickup styles for acoustic guitars. Other than certain clip-on and "soundhole" pickups, most of the better acoustic pickups are mounted inside the guitar or under the bridge saddle. Acoustic guitar amplification generally requires an input jack to be mounted in place of the strap button at the butt end of the guitar body. Leave the saddle slot-routing, end-pin-jack-drilling, and so on to the pros—it's too easy to ruin your guitar.

MAJOR REPAIRS

If you're looking at a serious repair job, get two or three estimates. See if a prospective repair shop can show you samples of its work—it's often surprising what you'll find (both good and bad). People have different ways of fixing things, and I sure wouldn't send a guitar to a shop without knowing what the staff was planning to do. A guitar tech shouldn't be insulted if you get other estimates.

If you're going to have your guitar set up, be sure to show the tech how you play—too often, techs will try to talk you into liking what *they* like. I've learned from experience to talk to customers about their preferences and playing style. That prevents a situation in which the customer comes back and says, "This buzzes," and I say, "Well, look how heavy you're playing."

Finally, keep a maintenance log. Write down who fixed your guitar, the date, and what was done. Ask the tech to list any materials—especially glues or finishes—that were used; such information can be invaluable in the future.

By the way: You can't have the lowest action in the world, light strings, and no buzz. Good luck! ∎

Loud & Proud

A ROCK GUITAR DISCOGRAPHY

This list points you to classic (and future classic) works by guitarists we explore in *How to Play Rock Guitar*. In creating their own styles, all of these artists built on tradition. So listen, learn, and then make the music your own.

AC/CD
(Angus Young
& Malcolm Young)
Highway to Hell
Back in Black (both on Atco)

Duane Allman
(w/The Allman Brothers
Band)
Idlewild South
At Fillmore East
(both on Polydor)

Paul Burlison
(w/Johnny Burnette &
the Rock 'n' Roll Trio)
*Rock 'n' Roll Trio: Tear It
Up*, BGO
Rockabilly Essentials,
Hip-O (various artists)

The Chantays
Two Sides of the Chantays,
Repertoire
*Rock Instrumental Classics,
Vol. 5: Surf*, Rhino
(various artists)

Eric Clapton
*Layla & Other Assorted
Love Songs*, Polydor
w/John Mayall:
*Blues Breakers with Eric
Clapton*, Deram

w/Cream:
Wheels of Fire, Polydor
Goodbye, Polydor

Dick Dale
*King of the Surf Guitar:
The Best of Dick Dale
& His Del-Tones*
*Rock Instrumental
Classics, Vol. 5: Surf*
(various artists)
(both on Rhino)

Fleetwood Mac
(Peter Green
& Danny Kirwin)
Then Play On, Reprise

Jimi Hendrix
Are You Experienced
Axis: Bold as Love
Electric Ladyland
(all on MCA)

Buddy Holobaugh
(w/Warren Smith)
*Ubangi Stomp: The Very
Best of Warren Smith*,
Collectables

Humble Pie
(Peter Frampton
& Steve Marriott)
*Performance: Rockin' the
Fillmore*, A&M

Korn
(Munky & Head)
Issues, Sony

Led Zeppelin
(Jimmy Page)
Led Zeppelin
Led Zeppelin II
(both on Atlantic)

Scotty Moore
(w/Elvis Presley)
The Complete Sun Sessions,
RCA

Pantera
(Dimebag Darrell)
Cowboys from Hell,
Atlantic
Vulgar Display of Power,
East West

Carl Perkins
Original Sun Greatest Hits,
Rhino

Queen
(Brian May)
Star Fleet Project, EMI
Jazz, EMI

**Rage Against
the Machine**
(Tom Morello)
Rage Against the Machine
The Battle of Los Angeles
(both on Epic)

Steely Dan
(Denny Dias
& Jeff Baxter)
Countdown to Ecstasy,
MCA

System of a Down
(Daron Malakian)
System of a Down, Sony

Eddie Van Halen
(w/Van Halen)
Van Halen
Van Halen II
1984
(all on Warner Bros.)

The Ventures
Surfing, GNP

Serious Players.

CMP
United Business Media

WHEN IT COMES TO MUSIC, WE WROTE THE BOOK.

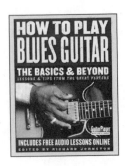

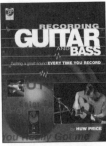